MISSION CRITICAL MESSENGERS

HOW TO DELIVER A DIFFERENCE

TRACY REPCHUK

with

Chelsea Krost | Martin G Edmondson | Precious Wilson | Keith Endow
Tricia Trimble | Adaku Ezeudo | Catherine Athans | Vanessa Standard
Yvette McDowell | Sally Landau | Veronica Anusionwu

Other Works with Tracy Repchuk

Start Right Marketing

31 Days to Millionaire Marketing Miracles

The Poetry of Business

Quantum Leap Your Life

Ultimate Life Lessons

25 Brilliant Business Mentors

Empower Business Everywhere

Mission Critical Messages

Discover more at
http://TracyRepchuk.com

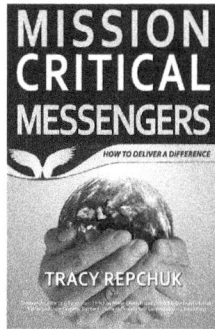

Mission Critical Messengers
How to Deliver a Difference

Tracy Repchuk

Co-authored with

Chelsea Krost ● Martin Gerard Edmonson
Precious Wilson ● Keith Endow
Tricia Trimble ● Adako Ezeudo
Catherine Athans ● Vanessa Standard
Yvette McDowell ● Sally Landau
Veronica Anusionwu

QuantumLeapAuthor.com

Published by QuantumLeapAuthor.com
Burbank, California

First published printing, March 2018

Editor: Marci Baun

ISBN-10: 0-9973036-1-1
ISBN-13: 978-0-9973036-1-2

Business & Money - International - Global Marketing
Business & Money - Business Culture - Work Life Balance

Printed in the United States of America

Cover Images: storybooks.com
Copyright: Innersurf International

For more information, or to order bulk copies of this book, please
contact QuantumLeapAuthor.com or
Tracy Repchuk at http://TracyRepchuk.com.

Acknowledgements

I would like to dedicate this book to those who know the journey is the learning and the destination is possible, and believe there is no mission that can't be met and no vision that can't be mapped!

This is for those who are ready to play a bigger a game, and reach for greater heights as you realize that one voice can change the world, and many can make a difference. No matter where you are in life, you have been through something, come out the other side, and need to tell your story. When you realize that making a difference isn't a desire—it's a destiny—you become a messenger.

In addition, I'd like to thank those who support the messengers—so we can lead, participate, and connect with amazing people, just like you. When we have support from family, friends, associates, mentors, coaches, mastermind groups, and followers, it gives us the luxury of time to do projects like this.

Special acknowledgements to those who have become leaders, visionaries, and deliverer of messages that took courage, persistence, perseverance and faith. For any names you don't recognize, please find out what they stand for or have accomplished.

Reverend Alfreddie Johnson, Bono, Grant Cardone, Jack Ma, Jeff Bezos, Joko Widodo, Ken Chenault, Malala Yousafzai, Martin Luther King, Jr., Nancy Lublin, Nelson Mandela, T.D. Jakes, Warren Buffet, Wendy Kopp.

Enjoy the book and connect with each of us!

Tracy Repchuk, 7 Time #1 International Bestselling Author and Speaker

Contents

Foreword

My name is Brian Smith, and as the founder of Uggs boots which is now a billion dollar brand, I can highly relate to the drive that is required in being a Mission Critical Messenger. There is no greater momentum that keeps you moving forward, keeps you on track to Deliver a Difference and keeps you plowing through barriers and obstacles than that desire to get the job done you were destined to do.

My journey was not an easy one, and sometimes you will find the fruits of your labor don't arrive when you expect, but if you persist beyond the reasonable, you will be rewarded when it was meant to be and when your lessons have been fully learned. In my book, *The Birth of a Brand*, there are guiding principles I live by which I wish to share with you now.

"You can't give birth to adults"—will help you understand that in your business you will move from tadpole on up and go through various stages that are critical for your learning and development, and to be patient as those unfold along your journey.

The four mantras I live by are:
1. Feast upon uncertainty.
2. Fatten upon disappointment.
3. Invigorate in the presence of difficulties.
4. Enthuse over apparent defeat.

This will keep you moving forward in times of uncertainty.

Then I want you to know "your disappointing disappointments will nearly always become your greatest blessing."

As you venture into become a messenger, someone who works hard to fulfill your destiny recall this, "Ignorance is a key element for every entrepreneur; some level of ignorance.

Because if you knew all the obstacles ahead, you would never do it."

And not to depress but to give you the confidence that if you are wondering why it's so hard, and thinking it's happening just to you, know this... "In life you get beat down. In business, you get beat down twice as much!"

But having truly committed, there this great ancient saying that says: Once you start on a path, the universe will conspire to work with you.

Decide, do it, and deliver your difference—no matter what —and you will always know you did all you could in the time you have.

Brian Smith
Founder of Ugg Boots

Chapter 1

The New Era of Philanthropy and the Part You Play
by Tracy Repchuk

For nonprofits. innovators, idea makers, and cause-based passioneers—the new landscape of technology is helping to make the world a better place. With crowdfunding becoming the norm for innovators and idea makers, it's time for nonprofits and its supporters to step up and play a bigger game.

In particular I am going to focus on how to help nonprofits grow and survive especially with government support on the decline, a tight economy, and an overwhelmed society with ever growing donation demands.

It's getting harder and harder to build and sustain a following... Until now!

I'm going to be talking about **How to Tap into the Goldmine of Online Givers** (that keep on giving).

So if you need more donors, promotion, and active members to increase the awareness and sustainability of your organization, then I'm going to share a secret with you.

Social media and online marketing have changed the landscape forever. It is more important than ever now to find effective ways to be heard above the noise, connect to conscious-minded contributors and convert them to raving fans that create an active community of repeat givers.

Before we start let me give you a bit of my background.

I have been involved with nonprofits since I started my first company in 1985 at the age of 19 where I leveraged technology so they could move their accounting in-house saving on average $5000 in data processing fees per month. Since then I have become a volunteer minister helping in disaster relief, a fully ordained minister, won awards from the Senate, Assembly, the White House and President Obama and I have **spoken in over 39 countries** and have experienced every technological change around the world for the past 32 years.

I've appeared on over 22 networks for TV including ABC, NBC, FOX, CBS, have over 13 published articles in Forbes, and I'm an invited member of the **Forbes Coaches Council** and have been featured in **three motivational movies**.

I have my own social tourism project called **GiveBack-Trips.com** and a 501c where trips to Vietnam to distribute clothes, education, food, and shelter happen to churches and orphanages across the country.

I'm a 7 **Time #1 International bestselling author** with Wiley Publishing, and what I do is help clients crowd fund for causes, plus do online marketing, social media strategy and done for you services for all online activities.

This has given me the ability to understand the issues that arise, especially when compounded with advancing technology - and how to grow, expand and nurture prospects to donors, and create a tribe and community of people that know, like and trust you, and how to create fundraising 'campaigns' that keep them engaged, active, sharing and giving.

So if you are among the millions of nonprofit organizations who find it all overwhelming and confusing, you will discover the 3 simple strategies to increase your donors, catapult their contributions, fast track fundraising, and capitalize on global philanthropy.

Today it's all about how to Make Giving Easier

We're going to cover 3 steps:
Conscious Connections
Conscious Communications
Conscious Contributors

Step 1 - Conscious Connections

The **problems** many nonprofits face are:
- Getting the Word Out About You and What You Do
- Finding the Money to Accomplish your Mission
- and Increasing your donor base

The solution leverages 3 key areas:
    (1) The first is social media and identifying where your target market is hanging out because you need to go where your crowd is, and leverage platforms such as Facebook or LinkedIn where you can nurture active and aware members. Social media—especially Facebook is designed to promote cause based solutions. I have one associate who promotes forgiveness and her own nonprofit on Facebook Live—and gets over one million views for a broadcast along with thousands of shares. Imagine that happening on your Facebook page.
    I have another client who uses Facebook Live to build his list and feed his crowdfunding campaigns with active members.
    Then you can add quote MEMEs, events, fun campaigns, and stay active, while followers share and help you get the word out. This is all free promotion.
    With over one billion members on Facebook, the

world of fundraising just got a whole lot easier.

In fact, Facebook is very dedicated to nonprofits and even have what's called a Social Good team.

However, since 66% of charities are worried that they will miss out on opportunities for digital fundraising—the key is to make sure you aren't one of them.

With the ability to set up your own Facebook page as a 'non-profit' you can then take advantage of fundraisers.

"Fundraisers" are dedicated pages where nonprofits can raise money for specific campaigns. The Donate button, previously reserved for ads on the site, will now appear on nonprofits' Pages and posts, allowing users to contribute directly from their News Feeds.

Then you can raise funds and awareness while creating relationships with tech savvy donors.

You can Easily Collect Donations now in a few taps without leaving Facebook and find new supporters.

Each time someone donates they are prompted to share and invite their friends. Shares and re-shares also contain a donate button making it easy to donate right from the newsfeed.

This simplicity encourages others to promote.

And, in this case, it can also showcase a progress bar toward its goal.

Any fundraiser shared by a user in a post will display the new donate button as well, allowing users to contribute through the post itself.

Followers can also easily promote and create their own fundraiser.

In 3 simple steps, they can create a fundraiser page (much like creating an event), select what they want to support, and select the nonprofit organization.

This gives your supporters a chance to set up a dedicated page to share their story, tell others about your mission, and rally around a fundraising goal.

Fundraisers give people the tools to get the word out through Facebook, Messenger, Live video, and email, all in a place their friends already visit every day.

(2) The second key area to consider is the Millennials

Millennials have become the largest generation in the workforce this year, and these moneymakers are more willing and likely to find you online and give via text or online more so than Gen Xer's or Baby Boomers. In fact, they are a generation focused on reversing the damages and issues that exist and are major contributors to cause-based crowdfunding campaigns.

1. One way is to establish a Millennial strategy and tap into this unique and growing demographic now.
2. Understand what your donors value and then determine how you can deliver that to them. Millennials love to share what they get behind so even if they don't become a giver, they may become loyal ambassadors for your cause.
3. Portfolio Structure - start to think in terms of helping them structure a giving portfolio so that consistent and recurring support can create long-term impact for what needs to be addressed.
4. Gratitude Gains the Giver
   The days of guilt have been replaced by gratitude.
5. Giving is a joyous gift to the giver and recipient and when your site, social media, web copy and promotion focus on that emotion, and you can begin to create a community that supports positive change in the world, and are appreciated for the part they play.
6. Tap into Tribes
   By creating online relationships, making it easy for them to share, give, and be a part of the fundraising

process, allows Millennials to form deep connections and feel valued.

(3) The third area to focus on is New Technology

Think mobile first. Creating a mobile specific site—not an app—can have you promoting the most important elements to savvy socialites at the speed of touch.

You also don't want to miss the boat on new technology that can help you reach a new audience or engage your supporters in a new way.

Instagram wasn't even on the radar five years ago, but is now one of the most influential platforms for nonprofits after Facebook.

Instagram is so effective for nonprofits because a picture is worth a thousand words.

You can use:
- Before and after images
- Human emotion filled photos
- Uplifting expressions
  It provides instant story telling with images that honor supporters, campaign goals, targets, accomplishments and you can
- Integrates with brand, talk about the staff, CEO, director, those you are helping
- Show and connect
  Then leverage the power of the # hashtag.

Both Twitter and Instagram heavily use the # hashtag feature which allows you to appear on other boards—broadening your reach and allowing you to engage in conversation. This is where you can reach millions in minutes.

Step 2 - Conscious Connections

The second key factor is Conscious Connections.

You see another issue facing nonprofits is not enough resources.

Entrepreneurs alike face this issue as they too operate on light staff and tight budgets. The remedy has become one of the greatest and most powerful additions—online newsletter and automated communications that convert followers to raving fans who help spread the word.

This is done with the addition of a new website called a landing page. It's only one page—but has a very specific purpose—and that is to capture the name and email of someone who is interested in what you do so you can automate the education process to the point where a new prospect wants to donate after understanding the scope of what you do.

In fact, when I have a client doing crowdfunding (which is a term that refers to any effort to raise money with donations from a large number of people over the internet), we create a landing page first that afterwards I have directing them to the donation opportunity via a thank you page and a video with a specific appeal to the current campaign. It gives a focused opportunity to direct their attention, appeal to their emotions, and leverage for many future campaigns.

So rather than expecting money right away, this creates a method of engagement or "conversations" that nurture and give supporters a chance to get to know your organization and build a deeper attachment to your work and mission. Then, by the time you're asking for cash, it isn't a hard sell.

The best part is it takes no additional staff effort once it's up and running and less staff for follow up, so tracking and converting donors is less about persuasion and more about relationship building.

By the time you hear from them, they are ready to donate.

To watch a video about landing pages go to <u>www. ALandingPage.com</u>

Step 3 - Conscious Contributors

The third step is to connect with conscious contributors.

Another issue for nonprofits I want to address is sustainability.

Solution - to get those that have already donated to give or refer more often.

Today's conscious contributors are tech savvy.

Much of the recurring donation growth has been driven by simplified online monthly giving, which was up 32 percent (compared to 9 percent for one-time gifts) on average.

Two additional focus areas are to shorten online forms so they display better on small screens and take advantage of auto-filling information stored on mobile devices.

This can make the donation process easier and smoother for your supporters.

Once you have these in place, you have the perfect formula to be ready for **crowdfunding.**

It is estimated to be a $96 billion industry by 2025, and a major source of funding for charities, nonprofits, and new ventures which Forbes states will be the next digital marketing frontier and currently is at the stage social media was 12 years ago.

This allows you to reach global audiences and raise money for anything from equipment, events, projects, and expansion. The sky is the limit with crowdfunding.

In fact, when I was a speaker in Las Vegas at this year's

Global Crowdfunding Convention, we honored Steve Sisolak who raised over $9 million dollars for the Las Vegas shooting victims in four days using the crowdfunding platform of GoFundMe and he started a trending #hashtag campaign called #VegasStrong which allowed him and others to keep this topic trending and front of mind for weeks.

With the power of these 3 steps aligned online (1 - 2 - 3)
1. Conscious Connections
2. Conscious Communications
3. Conscious Contributors
you can make giving easier and create real change for your organization, your donor and society at large.

LET ME HELP YOU WITH MY FREE GIFT!

Whether you are a non profit trying to create sustainability and growth, a speaker/author or coach that needs to elevate your status, or a business that needs moving into the online world in way that gets you seen, heard, making more money and reaching millions with your message in an impactful and streamlined way, I can help you.

If you are a non-profit, grab a copy of my free gift and watch a video training where I show you how to connect and convert prospects into donors.

Go to: www.MakeGivingEasier.com

If you want to create an online presence that elevates your status, authority and influence, and automate and streamline your sales and lead conversion process so you can create raving fans that catapult your cash flow—then schedule a call with me.

We can solve all your online problems such as;
- Cohesive branding and message match
- Online strategy for social media and lead capture
- Lead generation and conversion
- Email marketing and sales funnel development
- Web development and eCommerce solutions

Book call here: www.TracyRepchuk.com/calendar

If you are looking for a speaker who can educate, engage and take your event over the top—connect and book me for your next event.

Find out more at: www.BookTracy.com

Tracy Repchuk

Tracy Repchuk is an online marketing and social media strategist and speaker.

A seven-time international best selling author who has been an entrepreneur since 1985, she has helped thousands of clients get their message out around the world. She is also an internationally acclaimed speaker and motivator in over thirty-five countries. She keeps audiences engaged with her ability to break down complex concepts and turn them into formula based success.

Her first software business, which she started at the age of nineteen, still supports Fortune 100 companies. She has been nominated for awards such as Entrepreneur of the Year, Chamber of Commerce Business Woman of the Year, Coach of the Year and Stevie Awards for Business Mentor of the Year, received White House Presidential Award for Volunteer, State and Senate Awards, Provincial Volunteer and software development awards and has appeared in the International Who's Who in seven categories.

She graduated in Business Computer Systems and went on to receive a Certified Management Accountants designation. In 2007, Tracy won "New Internet Marketing Success of the Year" from the World Internet Summit and catapulted into success with her best selling book, speaking engagements, and extensive internet experience in web development, software integration, and marketing since 1994.

Tracy specializes in online marketing campaigns that build a cohesive corporate or personal brand using an integrated web strategy that helps you attract more leads, get more clients, and make more money. Her solutions are done with marketing and results in mind. In addition, she has appeared on TV: ABC, NBC, CBC, CTV, CBS, FOX, HGTV, 7 For Your Money, 4 On Your Side, WBZ, Report on Business Television, USA Today, Radio, magazine, newspaper and her work has appeared in over fifty publications including three motivational movies.

Chapter 2

5 Modern Marketing Tips to Master the Millennial Marketing Formula

by Chelsea Krost

Lazy, entitled, the demise of the future...LAZY, ENTITLED, THE DEMISE OF THE FUTURE. As I lay in bed (back in 2007) these words kept repeating in my head over and over again. Earlier that day I had caught a segment on *The View*, where my idol, Barbara Walters, was deep in conversation about, "The Teenagers," *this was before the term Millennial, those 18-35, was coined.* I was so taken aback by the negative perspective of my generation, and little did I know, that was just the start of it. After the negative chatter grew louder and louder, I began to seek out a platform that empowered us. After finding absolutely nothing, I decided to do something about it. I wanted to give my generation a voice. I turned frustration into determination to change the stereotype Entitled to **Entrepreneurial.**

And so, my mission began to create a platform that would bring teenagers together and challenge the misconception that this generation wasn't GREAT! Six months later, all my hard work and dedication paid off, my radio talk show concept, Teen Talk Live, got picked up on WBZT, a local am Clear

Channel station in South Florida. Today, my sixteen-year-old self would immediately think to create a YouTube series or launch an Instagram page, but back in 2007 that was a foreign concept and local radio was my opportunity.

Three years into hosting Teen Talk Live, I realized that the show was more powerful than I ever expected. I was amazed that just as many GenXers and Boomers were tuning in to understand their children and grandchildren's mindset, thought processes, and opinions. We were different...and older generations were, and still are, struggling to relate.

As social media, blogging, and influencers grew in popularity the needle started to shift and TV networks, newspapers, magazines, Fortune 500 companies, and businesses of all sizes got a wakeup call...what once worked in the past will not work in the Digital Age!

Now ten years later, and Millennials have officially outnumbered Baby Boomers and have the largest combined spending power of any generation. Yet, there are still misconceptions about this generation and confusion on how to master marketing to Millennials. Millennials', aka Digital Natives, needs and preferences are always evolving with developments in technology. But the first trick in garnering their loyalty involves getting their attention and keeping it, which is no small feat considering Millennial consumers aren't as likely as Gen-Xers and Boomers to respond to traditional advertising or marketing tactics.

Millennials are an economic force! With $200B in annual buying power, smart marketers know they need to use new channels to hook this generation. They are the least frequent in-store shoppers, the most responsive to online shopping opportunities, recommendations from friends and family, and are motivated by a seamless shopping experience. This generation learns how to DIY everything from YouTube videos, decides where to eat based on Instagram posts, plans their wedding with Pinterest boards, and has their groceries delivered to their door thanks to various mobile apps. YEAH, times have changed!

No need to scratch your head in confusion or throw your hands up in frustration anymore trying to figure out where to be and what to do to cut through the clutter. Here are 5 Modern Marketing Tips to Master the Millennial Marketing Formula:

1.   Focus on Audience Segmentation

One of the major appeals of Millennials as a target audience is that there are 80+ million of them out there. That's a lot of wallets and future consumers. The only problem is that there are many different types of Millennials with very different needs, pain points, aspirations and life circumstances.

Millennials are not a homogenous group and cannot be treated like one. The Millennial generation bracket is 18-35 years. That is a wide age range and the spending power, need, and mindset of a 20-year-old college student is different than a 30-year-old Millennial mom. Today, marketers are forced to look at real segmentation, based on age, culture, income and family structure.

By tapping into the six different age groups within the Millennial population, businesses can refine their strategies to appeal to each consumer segment. Take a look at the breakdown of the Millennial Micro Markets below.

6 Micro Markets within Millennial Generation.

1. College students: 18-23 years old

2. Boomerang Babies (young adults): 23-26 years old

3. Millennial Hustlers (aspiring entrepreneurs): 26-29 years old

4. Millennial mom & dad: 29-32 years old

5. Cuspers (Identify with Gen Xers): 32-35 years old

6. Millennials @ Heart (Gen Xers that relate to the Millennial Mindset): 35-38 years old

Pinpoint which age markets you want to target to create messaging and experiences that are tailored and valued by this audience.

2. Think Digital and Mobile First

This is the most connected generation in history, so if you're not targeting Millennials via smartphones and tablets, you're missing out big. According to, Media Post, a whopping 63% of millennials shop on their smartphones every day and 84% of millennials use smartphones in stores to assist with their shopping.

The last thing a business owner needs is to miss out on sales because their website and mobile website are not properly set up to provide the user a seamless customer experience. This tech-savvy group wants interactions that move seamlessly across multiple devices. Studies have proven that customers who don't buy online say it's because they find it too difficult to confirm product details. They're looking for detailed product specs and information, user reviews, and the ability to zoom in on high-definition photos. They want comprehensive instructions and FAQ videos that don't leave them saying, "This is too difficult or I don't get it!"

The question to ask yourself now is, "Is my website and mobile site working for me or against me?" Not sure? See how

Website Checklist for a Seamless Customer Experience

- ☑ Established Cohesive Brand Identity: Brand Logo, Message/Story, Copy, Voice, Colors, Product Placement.

- ☑ User Friendly Website Interface (SEO Optimized)

- ☑ Mobile Optimized Website

- ☑ Website Analytics Tool to Track User Behavior

- ☑ Customer Service Support: List Contact Information

- ☑ Online Reviews - Repurpose User Generated Content

- ☑ Quality Product Images and or Videos: How To Videos, Tutorials, Size Chart.

- ☑ User-friendly Shopping Cart: Provide clear shipping and return policy information.

- ☑ Appealing Email Opt-in

- ☑ Cross Channel Brand Presence (Your Digital Ecosystem)

- ☑ Social Media Widgets On Website

- ☑ Social Metrics Tracking Tool

chelsea

many boxes you check off from the list on the previous page.

3.   Invest in Social Media

For those who may have put off Social Media thinking it was going to be a fad with little impact on your ROI, there is so much data that proves that thought wrong!

According to Adroitdigital survey, 60% of Millennials reported that social media has the most influence over their perceptions of brands. Millennials also prefer brands that engage with them via social media, so a strong, interactive social media platform is critical. To roll out an effective Social Media Marketing Strategy, companies need to take the time to learn which social media channels and what content work best at conveying messaging, promotions, product, services, and brand personality to their target audience.

Just because Millennials are insanely active on social media, it doesn't mean that all social media platforms are worth your time or suit your brand. Each social media platform beats to its own drum, just like its users. Your social media strategy for Facebook will certainly be different than your strategy for Instagram. Why? Because each social platform attracts a different demographic within the Millennial population.

Leveraging social media is often presented as a way to increase brand awareness and engagement for free, which it is! But you won't see the needle move much if you don't invest time, creativity, and money into your channels. Yes, you can set up social media platforms for free, post content, incorporate hashtags, and LIKE other posts until your thumb gets sore. However, this won't generate the strong results that we all hope to achieve for our business.

Social media advertising can be executed with virtually any budget. Social media allows you to have an immense reach at a low cost. By utilizing paid social media advertising, you can reach an audience beyond your current followers and really start to see your follower count and engagement start to scale. You can get very specific with targeting, which allows you to reach consumers that will have a genuine interest in your brand.

More than half of US small-business owners anticipate increasing their social media budgets in 2018, and digital ad budgets are the highest they have been in the past decade. Allocating budget to social media advertising is a necessity, but this does not mean you should ignore consistently sharing organic posts. We can no longer put off social media. It is important for brands to find a balance between paid and

12 Things To Do On SOCIAL MEDIA

1. Share Everyday
2. Share Creative Posts About Your Products Or Services
3. Plug Content From Your Other Platforms: Repurpose!
4. Start A Discussion & Crowdsource Feedback
5. Share Company Milestones
6. Share Relevant Industry News On Your Feed
7. Start Contests For Your Facebook Fans and Poll your Twitter Followers
8. Reply to Fan Comments & Follow Others
9. Encourage and re-share User Generated Content
10. Update Your Fans About Upcoming Events And Promos
11. Discover and Use Proper Hashtags In Posts
12. Find Key Influencers In Your industry – Befriend & Engage!

organic—but plan on spending some extra time on finding where your target audience is and budgeting for a paid strategy and it will be worth it.

4.   The Power Influencer Marketing

The average person spends 100 minutes on social media every single day. According to emarketer, in 2016 ad blocker users increased from 69.8 million to 86.6 million internet users. These two factors alone have truly created a monumental shift in the marketing space and a demand for us to start thinking of innovative ways to capture consumer attention.

This is where the influencer comes in. Influencers are creating a big ripple effect in the social space and have become the ultimate authority on sharing What's Hot and What's Not to their followers. Influencers are entrepreneurs, content creators, thought leaders, and everyday people who have built a loyal and engaged online community. Change happens here. Eighty-eight percent of respondents in one survey said they trust online reviews the same as they do a personal recommendation. It is not just about tapping a big-name celebrity with a zillion followers to share one post on behalf of your brand. Instead, it is about aligning your brand with one stellar or several micro influencers who are proving to have the same—if not better—results. Influencer marketing content has been proven to deliver 11 times higher ROI than traditional marketing.

Influencers are passionate about a niche space *(fashion, food, fitness, finance, etc.)* and know what content speaks to their audience. The influencer and blogger community creates content that feels more transparent and authentic to consumers. Twitter users report 5.2 times increase in purchase intent when exposed to promotional content curated by influencers. It feels more like a recommendation from a peer than a celebrity endorsement and is ultimately more relatable. Simply, they know what products and messaging resonates best within their niche communities.

5.   Content Marketing

You must have heard the phrase *content is king*. Now, that may well be a marketing buzzword, but this year, it's a statement that has never been more relevant. In a world where consumers are savvier, more demanding, and more skeptical than ever, brands and businesses need to up their content marketing efforts to engage, inspire and convert. Content marketing is a strategic marketing approach focused on creating and distributing valuable, relevant, and consistent content to attract and retain a clearly-defined target audience. Ultimately, enhance awareness, encourage loyalty and increase profitability. Here are a few tips to take into consideration when crafting your content marketing strategy.

1. Branding is imperative for any company. Make sure you know what you and your company stand for and be consistent in your message. Millennials are a skeptical generation, so if they sense your message is inconsistent or phony, they won't feel connected with your brand and will be turned off.

2. It's no secret that the use of video in content marketing is on the rise. And, it's certainly not a tactic to be taken lightly. In fact, YouTube is now the second largest search engine on the web, video value demands a front-runner position in your content marketing plan. So, when you're considering what types of posts to schedule on social networks in the coming weeks, think video:

audiences are about ten times more likely to engage, embed, share, and comment on video content than blogs or related social posts.

3. Quality over quantity. Be thoughtful about the frequency of your marketing. Millennials don't want to be bombarded—if you're disseminating information too often, they'll feel like they're getting spammed and will be put off. On the flip side, however, they prefer brands that are active on social media and post regular content. So, make sure you're putting stuff out on a regular basis, but not so much that it's overwhelming.

4. Think about the seamless experience. In other words, your readers should be able to access your content on a desktop computer, then continue where they left off using their smartphone or complete their purchases through your mobile app, with absolutely no hassles at all.

5. Use data to drive your marketing. While there's certainly an aspect of creativity that goes into developing content, ignoring the data is a big mistake. Infographics are being used more, and more have been increasing in effectiveness. Data always tells a story and will guide you to the most effective methods of reaching your target audience.

Millennials really are a complex and unique generation. They truly are unlike any other generation before them, and their desires and preferences are always shifting and changing as technology evolves and advances. One thing is for certain, though, and is unlikely to change anytime soon: at the core, Millennials know what they want and what matters to them. They value being true to themselves, and they demand the same transparency in the brands they support. Brands and businesses that align with those values are the ones that will truly have the strongest staying power.

Are Millennials your target consumer? Have you given up on Social Media and feel unclear of what marketing strategies will cut through the clutter, generate traffic, and ROI?

I work with clients in various ways and have several options for turn-key and "done for you" solutions to fit your needs and budget. If you are Business Owner looking to understand Millennial consumer behavior, social media marketing, and how to boost traffic, engagement, and more sales online...then let's schedule a free Discovery Call to map out your plan of action together.

Where I Can Help
- Understand the Millennial Consumer Mindset
- Marketing Tactics That Convert Millennial Consumers
- Branding & Messaging Refinement
- Social Media Marketing
- Influencer Marketing
- Content Marketing
- Events: Keynotes, Influencer Panel, Video Production
- Traditional Broadcast & Digital Programing
- Public Relations
-

I'd like to give you a free copy of my "Millennial Marketing Formula Guide."
Head on over to MillennialMarketingFormula.com to take action now!

You Are Your Only Limit!

Chelsea Krost

Chelsea Krost

Chelsea Krost has had a passion for empowering Millennials since she was just 16. Today, Chelsea is one of America's leading Millennial influencers, Millennial marketing and brand strategists, keynote speaker, media personality, and the #MillennialTalk chat host. She has continued to evolve her business to provide unique services both in front and behind the scenes for small businesses, startups, and Fortune 500 companies like Intel, IBM, MasterCard, Kotex, vitaminwater, Cosmopolitan Magazine, and Capital One. At just 26 years old Chelsea has been rated by LinkedIn as a top Millennial marketer to follow and was inducted into the Forbes Coaches Council in 2017. For the past 10 years Chelsea has been the go to Millennial Expert for National TV shows like GMA, Today Show, CBS, FOX, CNN, MSNBC, Bloomberg, INC, and many others. Chelsea offers live coaching and online DIY programs, like her **Millennial Marketing Formula** course, to entrepreneurs and businesses of all sizes. She specializes in those who are looking to gain a deeper understanding of Millennial mindset, zero in on what to do on social media, explain how to use influencer marketing, streamline digital marketing strategies, and reveal how to build a loyal and engaged online community.

For more information visit: www.chelseakrost.com or www.millenialmarketingformula.com

Join me on social media: @chelseakrost

Chapter 3

The Write Stuff! The Life Hack to Writing a Screenplay in Under 30 days

by Martin Gerard Edmonson

So, I decided to write a screenplay.

First of all, I always loved writing. Well, except for those English assignments and book reports. What I loved writing about were my friends and our shared misadventures. We were a strange mix of oddballs, always looked over by outsiders. I would entertain them with stories and comic book style adventures where we were the heroes, and we would get the girl in the end. At that time of my life, the part of "getting the girl in the end", probably was the biggest stretch of reality. However, it made for good conversation by lit trash cans in the middle of a New York City park in the dead of winter. I wish I could say it was Central Park, but that would be lying.

Unbeknownst to most people looking at NYC from afar, there are many parts of the city, and many neighborhoods. I grew up in Washington Heights in the 1970's and 1980's. That neighborhood is located in the very northern tip of Manhattan. From afar, it would be labeled drug-ridden and crime-plagued. For me, it was the best of times, a magical time; it was my Neverland (Peter's not Michael's). I never had to go home; I never got ID'd at the bodega or the smoke shop. I could hang off the George Washington Bridge to write graffiti, mark my spot, and no one cared. I could buy beer in bodegas at 12 years old, the only requirement, put a bag on it! The whole bag thing changed after Giuliani, but that's another story. We would drink beer (40 ounces, of course), howl at the moon, and dream of fantastic futures, even if only for those cold nights with some of the greatest friends I ever knew.

Then I got older, joined the US Air Force, and learned responsibility, pragmatism. I abandoned my writing, not because of the US Air Force, just because... Those were dreams hatched in the middle of a winter's night, drunk with youth, and malt liquor! What sane person writes for a living? I managed to finish my Air Force commitment, go to Nursing School (Yes, Nursing School!), get married to the most beautiful girl in world, my Dominican Queen (AKA, my beautiful wife, life partner, lover and friend, Johanna), have three children. Janos the eldest, the graduate, botanist, and our inspiring artist, Jonas our loving, sensitive caring middle child, and future Oscar award winning film maker, and finally my greatest cheerleader, future military school graduate, and forensic scientist, my beautiful princess Jolin. For some crazy reason, my wife and I decided we should go to China, and adopt our fourth child, Joyel. For my next stunt, I nearly landed us in bankruptcy during the Great Recession trying to become the next mega real estate developer, then at the ripe age of 45 discover I had a story to tell, reconnect with the Repchuk's Tracy and Dave, and write the most groundbreaking manifesto on screenwriting that has ever been written. I mean, when this gets out to the public, I fully expect to find a copy of Mission Critical Messages right next to every Bible in a Hotel Room. They go together, like tacos and Tuesdays! Am I right?

So, I am not here to pontificate about my life, and experiences (too late, I know), with the exception of being a screenwriter. I am trying to provide some background to share where I came from, so you can see, don't give up on writing stories, or plays, or screenplays. It's what turns your switch that's important. That singular purpose is the reason you should be writing.

When you are writing, whatever the subject, does it move you? That's your focus when considering what you are writing about. What gets me is my insane sense of humor, and, if it makes me laugh, I keep it. If it makes me cry, I keep it. If it puts me to sleep, I read it every night, but never think about publishing it. You can do this, too, just follow the steps and start writing, even if you don't know rule one about screenplays. I didn't, and I managed to write a 187-page feature-length film screenplay that is currently being reviewed by producers.

Anthony Robbins, always says, "Success leaves clues!" I will summarize the clues to get you started; the rest is up to you! Own it and your responsibilities; own it, and you shall succeed in writing your book, your play, your screenplay! That's all that matters, I promise. Do you love your work? If you get someone else to enjoy it, God Bless, but be your own critic, and your own supporter.

Get out of your own head!

You may ask yourself, what do I know about movies? The people in Hollywood are experts! I'm just some dude, or dudette, tapping away at my keyboard. Yes, you are, and so are they. They just got out of their own head and started, and kept taking the next step, until, they got published, or had their screenplay bought. By the way, have you seen the garbage that gets released yearly out of Hollywood? I mean, come on already! I left one movie (*Gods of Egypt*) angry that I lost two hours of my life. I didn't even get a chance to think maybe this might be alright; no, it stunk from start to finish. So, let me tell you, I have some very big questions about their "expertise" in Hollywood. Let's agree, at the very least, you can write a very big budget film that can bomb just as quickly as any of the "experts". If you're telling me that is beyond the pale, please close this book and stop writing. Don't even write holiday cards.

Where to Start?

Start at the end. What? Yes, start at the end? What's this story about? Where are we going on this journey? Then reestablish your beginning. Where did our hero start from? Like building a bridge, you start from both sides of the river. Then fill in important turning points. Like posts that support the span of the bridge across the body of water, these will be where your story ties into and what allows your characters to move along their interesting journey, just as Dorothy did in *The Wizard of Oz*.

You are an expert

Think about the story that's running around in your head. Are there movies already made that remind you of it, or that you hope your movie could be like? If so, are there scenes in movies you love that you think the style or the wording are what you would want? Then you need to go to Google (sarcasm alert) and search: free screenplays. Choose your portal and download scripts from movies that you loved or that remind you of your scene or movie idea. Review the scenes that you are interested in and review how the author wrote his or her scene out. For now, just mimic the style and structure; apply it to your scene or movie. Notice how they write visually. The saying is, "If you didn't write it, you're not going to see it".

This is a scene from the screenplay I wrote: (it's an Alternative Rock Anime Musical based on the Romeo and Juliet story). (Don't laugh, it rocks!) *Star-Crossed Lovers* by Martin Gerard Edmondson and Karin Ursula Edmondson.

He turns towards him.

PRINCE JANOS

Yes indeed, brother.

LARGE OFFICER

Enough! Enough with your shenanigans, you are both going

to the Klink.

PRINCE JONAS

(Indignantly)

Do you know who we are?

SMALLER OFFICER

No, who?

PRINCE JANOS

(Janos interrupts before Jonas speaks)

The Kardashians, yes, we are the Kardashians!

PRINCE JONAS

(Interjects in a cracking, squeamish voice)

He is Kim. I'm Kanye.

They both fall out laughing. As they look up from their laughter, they notice the guardsmen from in front of Juliet's castle have surrounded them.

Don't have a clue one how to format a script in final draft.

Don't worry; start writing in Microsoft word, or whatever word processing software you prefer. Just mimic the structure of the scripts you did your research on. Then one of the biggest finds I discovered in my professional career was the website and services available on Upwork (Thank you Tracy, you sent your students there when it was called Elance). For $100 USD dollars, you can have an expert format your script so it looks like a professional script and will at least be taken seriously.

I recommend Final Draft Software for screenwriting mostly because that is what the industry uses. There are plenty of legal ways to buy a copy for less than retail. Places like eBay, Amazon, and dozens of other sites I am sure you can get a copy (generally, it runs around $100USD).

The First Draft

It's going to be rough, don't worry! Remember the three words in screenwriting.

Revise, Revise, Revise. Of course, followed by the other three words: again and again and again.

That is followed by (ALL TOGETHER NOW!) revise, revise, revise, etc. You know the drill! Remember, no sacred cows. If it works, keep it. If it's the greatest piece of literature that has ever been written, but doesn't fit in your story, sayonara, baby. No sacred cows...ever.

In between revisions, do something crazy like let other people read it. (No, your dog or cat or pet parakeet does not count.)

Let other people read it.
1. **Print out the copies.** Yes, I know it's going to be like half an acre of rainforest, but it's your career here. Then go plant some trees.
2. **Give it to people who actually read.**
3. **Get a professional Opinion**. Go to **The Blacklist**. Link: https://blcklst.com/
   - Professional Screenwriters Website for screenplay submissions.
   - $75 USD gets a professional industry reader to read your script and provide feedback. (Good feedback, not that, "Yeah, it was alright" kind of feedback that leaves you nowhere).

Rule of Thumb. When you get an 8/10 on The Blacklist, you can start shopping it. (That's a whole other story.)

Shopping your script.

You would think if it gets an 8/10 or better on somewhere like The Blacklist, you would have people beating down your doors. Well, that is not the case. You have to work to get your art in the hands of someone that may actually be able do something with it.

Hire an agent. It's not that easy. They want writers that have had success. Well, how do you get success if someone won't even read your script? And how do you get it in front of a reader if you don't have an agent? Well, agents, and managers, come later. You have to be your own marketer. That's why having people like Tracy and Dave Repchuk teach you how to market on the internet and social media is so vital.

You are your brand. The public and the screenwriting industry needs to see you as legitimate—a real writer. They have to take you seriously. That is why how you represent yourself on your website and on your social media outlets is so vital. Contact Tracy and Dave Repchuk for information on their marketing classes. (http://tracyrepchuk.com/).

A great little book you can get on Kindle is *Script Writing 101: Selling a Screenplay in the 21st Century* by Michael Rogan. Actually, this is the best resource that I have come across. It's up to date, funny, and full of clear advice and includes steps to market your screenplay, minus any fluff.

Use social media like Facebook, Twitter, Google Plus, LinkedIn, and My Space (in case you want to make sure you turned over EVERY stone). Remember, initially, it's a call to your current friends to just see if anyone knows someone in the film industry. Then add value. Post and tweets need to be funny, thoughtful, and most of the time about the writing / creative process, the other times, creative groveling (80/20 mix) to plead for help with your life's work. Keep testing, see what works, and stay with it. Rejection is part of the game. If it was easy, everyone would be doing it, and no one would find it interesting.

Give Blessings to Received Blessings

Remember the children story, *Stone Soup* by Marcia Brown? Its message was simple: alone we each have one small ingredient. If we all contribute our one small ingredient to the cause, then we can have a greater feast for all of us. The GOAL is a grand party, which we all share in and celebrate together. Remember, the value we bring is the value we receive.

Get together with a group of friends and throw a party, barbeque, or go to a local pub. Involve them by giving them parts in your screenplay. Have drinks and food, laugh with each other, film the table reads for your YouTube channel. It's a great marketing tool; your friends will want to share with their friends and family. Soon, it will take off; at the very least, you will have a great night with some good company.

In the Bible, Luke 6:38, the mantra is, "Give and thou shalt receive." This is a common theme in tapping the energy of the abundant Universe. Warning, it works both ways. Give bad vibes, get bad vibes. So, stay on the good side. Give, create, and be kind. It shall come back to you.

When posting, tweeting, texting, etc., are you creating or are you destroying? It's one or the other. Create, put out good energy, helpful energy, try to help someone else out there that is struggling in the writer's community. Share with them your story and struggles, and, most of all, how you got through it. You never know, your words and experience might be the one that unlocks it for them.

When marketing yourself or your script, give value to others, and they will reciprocate in return.

Let's stay connected!

BEST ORIGINAL SCREENPLAY

Fort Tryon Film Festival 2017
Antioche: Star Crossed Lovers

1. E-mail – martingerardwrites@gmail.com
2. Facebook Fan Page
   – www.facebook.com/martingerardwrites
3. LinkedIn - www.Linkedin.com/in/MartinGerardWrites
4. Twitter - www.Twitter.com/MartinGWrites
5. YouTube - www.YouTube.com/MartinGerardWrites
6. Google + - https://plus.google.com/MartinGerardWrites

Free Gift: Free Gift!

Just contact me at my e-mail Martin@MartinGerardEdmondson.com with a copy of your receipt for Mission Critical Messengers, and I will send you free screen writing software that is better than Final Draft Pro (and it's FREE!) (Really, this is not one of those Lucy pulling the football moments from Charlie Brown, I pinky swear!)

Martin Gerard Edmondson
screenwriter

Martin Gerard Edmonson

Martin Gerard Edmondson, is a US Air Force Veteran serving during Operation Desert Shield and Desert Storm (1990-1993). He has continued his dedication to veterans and their families as a Registered Nurse at the Bronx Veterans Affairs Medical Center. Martin has earned a Master's Degree in Nursing, specializing in Clinical Systems. In addition, he is a graduate of The New York Film Academy Screenwriting program. He has written 4 full feature length film screenplays, and has completed an additional 3 treatments for future films. He has been highly reviewed on the Professional Screenwriters website, The Black List. He won his first Film Festival Award for Best Screenplay at the 2017 Fort Tryon Film Festival. At this writing, his screenplay Star Crossed Lovers is currently in negotiations to be purchased by a Hollywood studio.

Using Principles from Life Hacks and Tim Ferris, The Four Hour Guru, he can show you how he started from absolutely no knowledge about screen writing to have written his first draft in under 30 days.

In addition, Martin Gerard Writes, is a blog and social media outlet that highlights events, articles and resources for screenwriters trying to get their films written and most of all made!

You can catch up to Martin Gerard Writes on Facebook, Twitter, Google +, LinkedIn, and YouTube.

Chapter 4

How to Get Paid to Sing
by Precious Wilson

I knew at an early age that your voice has a profound effect on how you can make someone feel, think, and act, and, from that moment, I knew I was a messenger.

Over the past 42 years, I have spent my time bringing joy into the lives of people all around the world, and now I bring to you six of the most powerful steps to help you use your voice too.

STEP ONE: SOUND MIND

The only thing that keeps you from getting what you want, is the 'story' you keep telling yourself as to why you can't have it.

The reality is that success begins by finding and adopting a success mindset.

When limiting beliefs and self-sabotage takes over, it begins to destroy your confidence and makes it difficult to get to where you want to be.

So, what are the conversations in your head that stops you?

Is it... Fear of failure? You're not good enough? Fear of rejection?

Here are some of the beliefs of people who fail:

You're afraid that there's too much competition. You're afraid that you tried once, it didn't work, so you gave up. You prefer the security of having a "proper 9-5 job ..." You're afraid that you'll become isolated, and that if you become successful, you'll alienate your family, partner, and friends.

BELIEVE IN YOURSELF

Being successful in life is all about how you handle those negative thoughts, it's about trusting yourself, that you are better than the moment, and having the proper belief system regarding who you are.

If you are unsure about who you are, then your dreams and goals would be less likely to become a reality.

For example, if you truly believe that you are "the best singer in the world," you would behave differently, compared to "I hope I'm good."

You would speak in a totally different tone of voice, your conversations would be more positive, you would walk differently, confidently and more relaxed.

We all have moments of doubt from time to time, even the most successful people that you admire and look up to, but the difference is that they don't "live there."

So, believe in yourself; that you have something special to offer the world and that you are worthy and deserving. Dreams have no expiry date.

STEP TWO: YOUR SIGNATURE SOUND

Singing is one of the most enjoyable and captivating ways

to express yourself.

The great thing about singing is the sense of freedom and pleasure that it gives both you and the listener.

The most exciting and mesmerizing voice is not always just down to talent alone. Often, it is the result of a burning desire, practice, perseverance, the right vocal technique, and emotional and physical health.

I must warn you that developing your own singing skills takes time and lots of practice, so if you haven't sung for a while or you're a beginner, you will need to start working on building your voice gradually.

Here in this second section, I'm going to walk you through a quick overview, of three fundamental building blocks to help build and develop your voice.

They are: **Posture**, **Breathing**, and **Warm-Ups** for your voice and body.

My advice is not meant to replace professional or One on One private coaching.

Please note that my tips are for those of you singers who are interested in contemporary, non-classical singing style.

POSTURE

Let's begin with your posture; your body loves alignment!

Stand up straight – imagine a string pulling you up from the top of your head.

Align your body. Your ear, shoulder, and hip should form a straight line whether seated or standing. Your feet should be hip-width apart, keeping your knees "soft" not locked.

Neutral Head Position. Glide your head forward as far as it will go. Then keeping your head level, glide it back pulling your chin down slightly, without dropping down. Gently release your head to a position in between, so that your ears are aligned with your shoulders. Look straight ahead, keeping your shoulders down. Try to relax, as tension will prevent you from making a good sound.

By the way, did you know that poor posture, actually accelerates the aging process?

Slouching around is another thing that causes the spine to shift from this normal alignment. Bad posture often results in pain and fatigue and possibly spinal degeneration and a permanent deformity.

When you stand tall and strong, not only is it better for your body, but it also helps you to exude strength, character, confidence, and authority.

BREATHING

We all know how to breathe for everyday activities, but there is a lot to be gained with effective management of your breath as this can result in better vocal control, increased vocal power, and it also improves your stamina. Developing good breathing techniques for singing takes practice and patience:

Inhale

Here's what you can do standing in front of a mirror: Imagine a rubber ring around your waist that expands all the way round your body, including your back. Take a deep breath in from your lower lungs. Breathe in through your nose and out through your mouth, and as you breathe in, try to push the ring outwards. Avoid raising your shoulders as you breathe in – keep them relaxed and level.

Exhale

You need the breath to sing, and so as you breathe out while singing your abdominal muscles contract slightly, this causes your diaphragm to arch up against your lungs,
Pushing the air out of your lungs.
A Simple Breathing Exercise to Try:
Lie on the floor on your back with your hands resting on

your stomach. Breathe in (inhale) and your hands will rise. Now breathe out (exhale) and they will lower.

In this position, it is virtually impossible to breathe incorrectly. Try to breathe in the same way as you would when you sing.

WARM-UP YOUR BODY

Singers are like athletes: they need to warm up before they perform.

Stretch 1: Spine Stretch

Start with physical warming-up and stretching your body, before your vocal warm-up. This will help your body to be more open and less likely to hurt yourself.

Stretch 2: Shoulder Stretch

Lift one arm above your head; bend your elbow so that your fingers point down along your spine. Using your other hand take hold of your elbow above your head. With your fingers pointing down your back, exhale slowly, and gently pull down on your elbow. Repeat on the other arm.

Stretch 3: Shoulder Rolls

Hands by your side standing upright. Raise your shoulders up to your ears. Roll your shoulders forward. Then roll the shoulders back and down continuously. Move in a smooth continuous motion up and backwards, and then return the starting position.

VOCAL WARM-UPS

Here are three of my favorite sounds to warm-up the voice. Try these before doing more structured scale work and detailed vocal technique.

Lip/Tongue Trills

A bubbling sound made with lips or tongue. This exercise is really helpful as it encourages you to relax the jaw and requires that you keep the air flowing. Both of these techniques help with free tone production.

Sliding or Siren Sounds

Moving your voice up or down, gliding continuously, in a perfectly smooth way. Vocalize through a series of pitches, without stopping, on any particular scale notes. Imitate the sound of a siren. You can use any vowel or just hum.

Humming

While keeping your teeth slightly apart, close your lips, hum a tone; you will notice a buzzing feeling in the lips, nose, and cheeks. You can also use with sliding up and down as in the siren exercise. The buzzing sensation the results when humming will increase your awareness of resonance. Resonance makes the voice sound louder, adding a variety in tone, making the voice brighter, better projection, and generally more interesting.

If you haven't done much singing before, it is particularly important to make sure you warm-up properly.

Just like you shouldn't do strenuous exercise without stretching your muscles, you shouldn't try to tackle a song without stretching your pipes.

Never strain your voice. If you feel tired, stop. Don't risk damaging your voice.

Do your best to maintain a healthy balanced lifestyle, in mind body and spirit.

One last thing, if you're really serious about your singing career, get yourself a good mentor and vocal coach... you're worth it!

STEP THREE: PERFORMANCE PITCH

There are singers, and then there are SINGERS!

If you wish to be successful in the music industry, your ability to perform on stage is a skill that you should master.

One of my favorite performers is Whitney Houston. I love the richness and the effortless beauty in her voice.

A truly wonderful vocalist who could make a nursery rhyme sound great.

But an important contributory factor to her success is that all of her hit songs were chosen with her specific voice in mind. Every aspect was tailor made to maximize her vocal strength and minimize her vocal imperfections.

So, choose your songs carefully so that you can communicate the message of the song.

STAGE FRIGHT

Stage fright is often a big problem for a lot of people, and *you're not alone.*

As long as there have been performances, there has been stage fright. Thousands of performers have experienced the nauseous, uneasy feeling in your stomachs, shaky hands, and much worse, before getting on stage. So, don't worry. It's not only you, because not only is it a common problem, but there is a solution.

Life is ten percent what happens to you and ninety percent how you respond to it.

Feeling good about your stage performances is all about mindset.

Reframe the Situation

Reframing is a great mindset technique to use when you

need to look at a situation in a new light.

Wrap Your Emotions

When you're performing, you tend to feel emotions such as fear and anxiety, either before or during a performance. One way to use reframing is to "wrap" your fearful emotions with positive ones. Try it and see!

STEP FOUR: MARKET MASTER

Getting Started

How do you get started in the music business as a performing artist or songwriter?

Create A Buzz

How do you get noticed? The idea is to create interest, a buzz by whatever means you can.

Find your venues to do live work. Tailor-make your material to your audience.

You can make a demo of your performances, or songs, and post it on a website like Soundcloud for peer approval. Translate your story into a newsworthy hook.

Your Demo

For most people, making progress in the music business means having a demo recording of your work. It should be recorded to the best standard that you can.

Think about your image - Create Your Own Style

The reason many singers have done so well is because they've created their own style and used it to their advantage. It's not always about being the sexiest or best-looking act in the industry although that can help; it's about having a style that reflects your personality and stands out.

If you are a beginner, you can ask your voice coach what kind of style would suit you. Once you've found your brand, use it on all your marketing materials.

Consistency Is Key

Your image is the thing that sells you when you're not singing. Therefore, making sure your consistent with all aspects of your brand is essential, from the logos on your artwork, to your social media, to your outfits and promotional material. You want the public to recognize your brand instantly, if they click on your website or your Facebook page it should be obvious they're on the right page.

Get Yourself Out There

The best way to find your image is to physically go out, perform and see what you're comfortable with. Playing at regular gigs will give you a sense of what you're comfortable wearing and what songs get you a good response. This experience will help you to develop yourself as an artist.

STEP FIVE: PEAK PROMOTION

Social marketing is here to stay, so it is important that you are effective in the way you use your social network platform. An online community of social network users can make or break you as a singer—users can spread the word about your music, and provide and share positive feedback about your music and performances. You are not selling yourself; you are creating relationships through communities.

Effective use of social network platforms ensures that, with the correct marketing strategy, it can help you build a positive and effective fan base.

Ideally, every singer should have a website as the hub of their social media platform, which all their social media account points towards, as that can host all of your content (music, videos, pictures, and news). However, as websites can be expensive, the next best thing you can do is to set up a blog on a platform such as WordPress or Tumblr.

Blogging is an important social media for singers as it provides your fans with an insight to your world. The overall purpose of your blog is to communicate exclusive information, ideas, and subjects with your target audience, and getting your readers responding and interacting back with you.

The key to effective social media for singers is synergy, making sure that all your profiles are the same and link up. This means having the same display pictures, backgrounds, and names for each social media profile.

STEP SIX: HOW TO GET PAID TO SING

When it comes to getting gigs, the first thing you've got to look at is how to be more *performance attractive* by standing out in the musicians' marketplace.

One of the secrets of attracting lots of performances to you is to stand out big time, be unique, and offer things others don't.

There's a standard marketing term called the USP, Unique Selling Proposition, that's going to be very important in helping you figure out why they should hire you as opposed to the other musician down the street.

It is crucial for you to identify and communicate whatever sets you and your music style apart from others.

Imagine a booking agent is looking through a list of singers in your category. How would you stand out? What would make them call YOU as opposed to the next musician?

Take a moment and answer these questions to help you form your USP as a performer: Of all the people in my field, what do I do, that others do not? What features of my music style sets me apart from others? What benefits can I promise that others do not? Why should a prospective venue manager or other musicians work with "me" as opposed to the singer down the road?

Your Team

You should start thinking about putting your team of advisers in place as soon as you start to get a bit of a "buzz" about you so that you are ready to move quickly. Your accountant and lawyer are vital members of your team. Don't rush this process; take your time to choose the right ones.

This is broad overview of how to create your path to success. If you would like me to guide you and help you with your vision and goals for your singing career, then connect with me here to find out more of my offerings.

The Vocal Touch
with Precious Wilson
Creating Your Path to Success in the Music Industry

What's next...

I invite you to opt-in and connect with me. I look forward to finding out more about your vision, purpose and mission, and help you achieve success in YOUR singing career.

Get Your Free Gift:

Head to: www.SingingCareerSuccess.com

Once you have joined my community you'll find an opportunity to get on a call with me.

On it, I can help you to determine what your next best action is to get the greatest results in the shortest amount of time.

I'm excited to connect with you, and I look forward to being a part of your journey in achieving success in your singing career.

What are you waiting for?

It's Your Time to Shine!
Precious

Precious Wilson

Precious Wilson

Precious Wilson started her singing career as lead singer with the soul disco group called Eruption. They covered the Anne Peebles classic "I Can't Stand the Rain". This was followed by "One Way Ticket", another gigantic international-al hit in both Eastern and continental Europe. Her solo single entitled "I'll Be Your Friend", underlined her appeal on the dance soul circuit and she reached the Billboard R&B Charts a second time.

Precious continued her success with the title track to the blockbuster movie starring Michael Douglas, Kathleen Turner and Danny De Vito, entitled: "The Jewel of the Nile" written by the team of Britten and Lyle who wrote Tina Turner's smash hit "What's Love Got TO Do".

She toured the former USSR on the invitation of the Soviet Cultural Ministry, and was the first black UK based female artiste to have undertaken such an extensive tour in the then USSR.

Her musical legacy is that of being one of the pioneers of the UK Black music revolution of the late 70's and 80's, alongside such artists as Junior Giscombe, Jazzy B (Soul 2 Soul), Heatwave, Loose Ends, and Eddy Grant.

Live performances, guest appearances, vocal contribution and collaborations include shows in the Albert Hall, Monte Carlo, the Kremlin, a Royal Variety Show in the presence of HRH Queen Elizabeth of the UK, a member of the Saudi royal family, James Brown, Boney M, Michael Bolton, Little Richard, Sir Cliff Richard, Sir Paul McCartney, and Sir Elton John.

Chapter 5

Your Real Estate Wealth
by Keith Endow

Longevity and improved health, compared to centuries past, has led to a greater need for more resources to assist us throughout our life. We enjoy a more enriching life when we include inspiration, mental and physical health, financial health, and other resources to meet both the expected and unexpected events of our lives.

I live on the West Coast of the United States in Southern California. Real estate has proven to be a resource for building wealth and sheltering some income, but there are details you need to know in order to gain wealth through real estate.

How can I help you build wealth so you can enjoy your life more fully, especially considering we never know the length of our lifespan, the sustainability of our health, or what may happen to our loved ones? I'd like to help you as much as I can when it relates to real estate strategies.

You must understand that, as my commercial real estate mentor used to say:

"You realize your profit when you buy, not when you sell."

This should be your baseline when you consider investing in real estate, and when you sell it as well. When buying a property, the details are important:

- the terms of the loan
- the amount of time to do your due diligence from inspecting the building and land to going to the municipal planning department to see the future zoning and use of the property of interest
- evaluation of comparable properties
- evaluating any adjacent property development plans
- additional details that may impact the value of the real estate and strategy for profit

You will find "Helpful Links" on the Real Estate Network website:

http://keithendowrealestatenetwork.com/helpful-links

Here you will find residential and commercial links to zoning information for the City of Los Angeles, as well as many other real estate resources.

Of course, it is best for you to go down in person to the Los Angeles City Planning Department and meet the staff. However, the information gained through the links will help you prepare for your meeting or conversation with the staff and other strategic discussions you may have, such as with your contractor or architect. Learn their language—this will be beneficial to you.

BE PREPARED

Whether buying or selling, you must be prepared.

If you are selling a property, you need to be proactive and anticipate any concerns that a buyer would have about your property. In line with realizing your profit when you buy and not when you sell, you as a seller have to make it easier for a buyer to see the upside in the property's value. Sometimes, it is better to delay putting the property up for sale until you have covered as many issues a prospective buyer may raise during the buying process. Examples may include: waiting for rezoning to be complete, waiting until the roof is certified as lasting more than 5 years by a licensed roofer, having a plumber confirm that the sewer line is free and clear of debris, etc. By doing this, the buyer will have confidence that they won't run into extra expenses to operate the property. These details can make the difference between closing on time or costing as much as $100,000 in expenses because a buyer was ready for a quick sale as long as the property was in good working condition.

You will see in the following example that the readiness of those involved in a huge land sale was important for its completion and for the transfer of title.

Consider the biggest real estate deals in United States history—the "Louisiana Purchase". Valued at $15 million dollars in 1803, after paying off the financing in 1823, it was called at $23,313,567.73 according to the Library of Congress.

Why was this one of the best real estate deals? As defined in Wikipedia: "The Louisiana Purchase was by far the largest territorial gain in U.S. history, stretching from the Mississippi River to the Rocky Mountains. The purchase doubled the size of the United States." It was considered to have reinforced the independence of the United States and helped its standing as a powerful nation in the international community. It also increased the freedom its citizens had to transport their goods and receive the along the Mississippi River.

What can we learn from this historical example? Good

negotiations are mandatory for good purchases, but only when you are prepared. Great purchases become more probable when you prepare an adaptable strategy to anticipate unexpected events. However, you must also have the power to execute decisions in order to be able to control the property desired.

Let's examine a few details for this historic real estate sale, then see how, with your own financial goals defined, you can create your own financial future and the building of real estate wealth.

For the United States to buy the Louisiana territory from France, the financing was set up with $3 million in gold, and the ability to finance the rest ($12 million) in bonds from several foreign banks. Instead of buying just areas for the safe passage of goods, the United States purchased land that later was divided into six states and portions of nine others. They not only knew the details of the sale terms, but also the political areas of support and the actual physical boundary details of what land they were buying. These details gave the United States the negotiating power, as they were able to quickly set up financing even though it was not all cash.

A more recent large real estate deal took place here in California concerning water rights for the benefit of the City of Los Angeles. The building of the original aqueduct that initially covered 233 miles was the world's longest in 1931. This project cost over $23 million dollars, and, like the Louisiana Purchase, it was generated by a bond financing. Between his bond fund and the initial bond in the amount of $1.5 million, it was a $24.5 million deal. Of course, this does not include the increase in land values and additional tax revenues that the City of Los Angeles received from the construction and water rights negotiated. We are still receiving the benefits from this agreement and subsequent deals.

These are two examples of historic real estate transactions.

My hope is that we can develop your real estate strategies to make history, too.

You have many business opportunities. Make the most of every opportunity by equipping yourself with current information and a strong network of resources, such as our real estate network of professionals.

It is not just financial opportunity, but as you may have already experiences, emotions, perceptions, and the people who advise you in developing the details of your real estate agreement affect its outcome. To minimize failure or loss, my experience says to look at real estate as a long-term investment.

Short period of ownership or control, such as a lease, should be looked as an exception rather than the rule. I use the word "control" because there are times you have control of a property or gifts to the use of a property (a lease agreement, an easement or option to purchase or extend a lease) and this control can be converted into money if there is demand to buy it or if someone has a need for it.

HOW TO START

I have created a basic questionnaire "Questions" on my website:

http://keithendowrealestatenetwork.com/questions

that will challenge you and your real estate goals. After you have summarized your real estate goals and calculated the amount of risk you are willing to accept to pursue to achieve these goals, we look for your desired property or locations. Other details will include what type of property best fits your style of management, or how much time you plan on dedicating for the monitoring of your real estate investment. This is where partnerships can benefit you and others depending on what talents and experiences they have. I have found that when you put your investment details in writing, you can better assess the type of properties and locations you seek.

Afterwards, you can assess what these properties are worth to the general market and what its value is to you under your investment requirements. The investor who is ready will be able to act quickly to capture this investment opportunity.

DYNAMICS

What dynamics can you apply now or for your future? Do you want to build wealth and create resources for future benefit? Regardless of your age and financial net worth, there are opportunities to consider. Not all profitable real estate related transactions involve just the buying and selling of real estate. For example, I was able to benefit from what we called a "sandwich lease", which is leasing a property from one person and then leasing that same property to another party for a higher amount. So, the master lease and sub-lease are the "bread", and the "meat" is the net profit (profit after cost of the lease and any other obligations of the lease terms, such as maintenance which was the case with my deal). Thus, a nice real estate "sandwich" created a nice cash flow.

Mark Cuban, a billionaire according to Forbes, wrote in his local paper, The Dallas Morning News, his advice to a lottery winner of a $1.6 billion jackpot:

"If you weren't happy yesterday, you won't be happy tomorrow.
It's money. It's not happiness.
If you were happy yesterday, you are going to be a lot

happier tomorrow.
It's money. Life gets easier when you don't have to worry
about the bills."

RELATIONSHIPS MATTER

The Louisiana Purchase by the United States would not have been possible without understanding the French culture and being aware of what and who influenced the seller. This historic international real estate transaction was achieved between people, just like today. The real estate business is a "people" business. Dealing with properties will differ around the world, but it is still dependent on people and their mindsets, their visions for the control of space, and goals they have for themselves and the institutions or family wealth they manage.

Why does this involve a Los Angeles real estate professional? Because, with over three decades of real estate experience involving all types of people and properties, I can use this knowledge and intuition for positive results.

Whereas the Louisiana Purchase involved rights of way for shipping, real estate clients are interested in other rights such as water rights, access rights, and permission to build a certain size or particular use building and parking. As Los Angeles is a global metropolis from its ports to its manufacturing and farming to its movie studios, it has the volume and range for any type of real estate transaction. (View opportunities at http://www.wtcla.org/industries) Whether you are negotiating with your life partner to buy a certain property or negotiating with a seller of a property you want to purchase, you need to know what motivates them. (Remember you need to know what your goals are and how much you want to risk initially and for the future. You are not just looking at risk, but returns and benefits.)

I help people build wealth and have a greater grasp of the many options they have available to them. There are economic cycles, both locally and globally, that could affect the decisions you make. Get good advice from trusted sources like your accountant, business partners, and other advisors. Then use fresh data that you understand to make your final decisions. Revise as you become aware of new information. Likewise, be open to consider old information with a new understanding.

Anyone can have data, but having information that specifically pertains to you and your situation will help provide the confidence you need to be at peace and enjoy this wealth building journey. Working with a network of resources provides greater empowerment—and this is how we desire to serve you.

LEARN MORE

To learn more about the aspects of real estate, and how to learn how the value in a property can be improved, go to: www.KeithEndowRealEstateNetwork.com. Here you will find a good start on ideas for both residential and commercial properties. We are always eager to answer any questions you may have, select Contact Us and we will be in touch, or call me directly at 1-310-722-2562.

KEITH ENDOW
THE REAL ESTATE NETWORK

Receive a complimentary 20-minute consultation (a $125 value) by contacting us for a free questionnaire and consultation appointment.

Visit: http://keithendowrealestatenetwork.com/contact-us

Submit the contact form. We look forward to being in touch with you soon.

Keith Endow

Born and raised in West Los Angeles, Keith knows Los Angeles and the surrounding areas inherently; an asset for those exploring the area for residence or business.

Keith began his real estate career at age 19 years, when he obtained his real estate salesman's license. Two-and-a-half years later he obtained his real estate broker's license.

Initially motivated by a personal goal of acquiring money for his recreation of skiing, Keith learned how expanding his viewpoint and raising his expectations could raise the level of income and profit. In 1977, he sold a 3 bedroom, 1 bath home for less than $50,000. A few years later, he was selling properties double this value. Each year, he progressed in variety and size of the properties sold, including a mortuary property at the foot of MGM Studios in Culver City, Montclair Shopping Center, Mar Vista estate lots and 3-story homes, Pico commercial and office near Koreatown, and many more.

Keith pursued additional growth in the real estate industry, so he moved to Newport Beach to learn commercial real estate development with a friend. Home sales were slowing down by 1979, as interest rates were high along with double-digit money market account rates. Expanding his knowledge and experience to include commercial properties looked like a good idea.

Now, Keith has brought his commercial real estate services back to the West Los Angeles area. As one of the top agents in

Los Angeles over the years, Keith has worked with some of the larger reputable residential brokerage firms such as Coldwell Banker, Prudential California Realty, and currently Berkshire Hathaway Home Services California Properties.

He has also benefited from working with boutique residential and commercial brokers, such as Bud Petrick and Associates in the 1990's, based in the Pacific Palisades, California, managing their West Los Angeles branch. He has worked as an independent broker during some seasons of his real estate career, selling a shopping center and managing it, along with other properties.

Although financial progression was valued, through his experience, Keith began to see a deeper source of fulfillment through the success of his business: helping people. This is done not only professionally, but for over 20 years Keith has volunteered with Meals On Wheels West delivering fresh meals to elderly and homebound residents enabling them to continue to live in their own homes. He has delivered meals to a spectrum of people from those in small apartments to larger, well-established residences. Keith states, "We all need each other, and it promotes health to be empowered by some independence which Meals On Wheels provides for their clientele. They make it easy to contribute to their volunteers, too."

He finds much satisfaction as he helps people build wealth and become aware of the many options they have available to them for a brighter future.

Following his vision and passion to help his clients to be best equipped, Keith hosts a website to serve:

www.KeithEndowRealEstateNetwork.com

This website is a Resource Destination for simple concepts and real answers to your real estate needs.

Chapter 6

Mineral Sunscreen: Your Best Anti-Aging Investment
by Tricia Trimble

The Role of Discernment

Did you know that up to 90% of visible skin aging is caused by sun damage?

Or that 1 in 5 people get some form of skin cancer in their lifetime?

So if you want to keep your skin youthful and protect yourself from skin cancer, doesn't it make logical sense to wear sunscreen?

Well, yes, but then... did you know that recent studies indicate many sunscreens can cause endocrine disruption and harm the wildlife in our ocean?

And on top of that, up to 85% of adults are Vitamin D deficient and being in the sun is what your body needs to create Vitamin D?

Oh my goodness...with all of this contradictory information, what are you supposed to do?

This was my dilemma. To top it all off, I have an increased risk of skin cancer due to family history, fair skin and light eyes.

I needed a solution so I created Suntegrity, a safe and natural mineral sun care line made in honor of my mom who passed away from melanoma skin cancer. The brand began in 2010 when I launched our first product as part of a Healing of Grief project for a Masters program I was in at Santa Monica University.

After losing my mom to skin cancer, I was left with a lot of pain and grief that I stuffed away into a hidden inner compartment that I never dealt with until this project. Since then, it's been my mission to help prevent anyone else from losing someone they love to skin cancer unnecessarily.

It's my belief that a lot of skin cancer and premature aging can be prevented with education, awareness, and an easy to apply product called sunscreen...but not just any sunscreen, one carefully crafted with effective and safe ingredients.

In this chapter, it is my intention to share with you what I know about sunscreen in hopes it will help you stay safe in the sun.

What is sunscreen?

We all know that it's the white creamy stuff (and sometimes tinted) that our parents were always yelling at us to put on before we left the house. But, have you ever wondered how it actually works?

Sunscreens are filters of UV energy. They are used to filter out a portion of the sun's UV rays before they penetrate your skin and cause damage.

Do sunscreens block out all UV rays?

No, sunscreens are filters not "blocks". All sunscreens let some UV radiation through at varying rates indicated by the SPF number. This is why the term "sunblock" is prohibited for use by the FDA.

What is the difference between UVA rays and UVB rays?

UVA light rays are long wavelength (320 – 400 nm) light rays and can penetrate into the deeper layers of the skin. Unprotected exposure to these rays can lead to premature skin aging (aka: photoaging) and wrinkles and may initiate the development of skin cancers. UVA rays are present during all daylight hours all months of the year and can penetrate through glass and clouds.

UVB light rays are the mid-range wavelength (290 – 320 nm) light rays and are responsible for tanning or burning the superficial layers of your skin. They also play a key role in the development of skin cancer. These rays are strongest between 10 am – 4 pm.

An easy way to remember the difference between the two types of UV rays is to think of "A" for Aging and "B" for Burning.

What SPF means and why it's important to know.

SPF (Sun Protection Factor) indicates how long you can stay in the sun without burning from UVB light rays. SPF *DOES NOT* indicate any protection from the damaging UVA rays.

For example, an SPF 30 product allows 1/30th of the sun-burning UV radiation energy through to your skin versus wearing no sunscreen at all. Wearing an SPF 30 product will give you 30 times the protection before burning takes place.

An SPF15 product blocks about 94% of UVB rays; an SPF

30 product blocks about 97% of UVB rays; and an SPF 45 product blocks about 98% of those rays. Most dermatologists recommend an SPF of 30 because the difference in protection above that is minimal, especially considering no SPF number will block out 100% of the rays.

What does "Broad Spectrum" mean and why should I look for it on my sunscreen bottle?

The term "Broad Spectrum" indicates that the sunscreen protects you from UVA rays. Since UVA rays are associated with aging and skin cancer, it is very important that you choose a sunscreen with "Broad Spectrum" protection or else you will only be protected from UVB rays.

Chemical (organic) & mineral (inorganic) sunscreens explained.

When you see the term "organic", don't be fooled. Sunscreens contain filters that either reflect or absorb UV rays, and there are two main types: organic and inorganic. Understanding the difference between these two categories often proves tricky for most consumers, who believe that the label "organic" (usually indicated by a USDA organic symbol in the food industry) denotes a healthy, safe product containing limited or no pesticides. However, when used in reference to sunscreens. The term organic means something entirely different. It is chemical terminology that simply indicates a substance contains carbon.

Chemical (organic) Sunscreen - Organic sunscreens *absorb* UV radiation and convert it into heat. Organic sunscreens contain one or more of the following ingredients: oxybenzone, avobenzone, octisalate, octocrylene, homosalate, octinoxiate.

Mineral (inorganic) Sunscreen - Inorganic sunscreens (aka "Chemical-Free", Natural Sunscreen) reflect and scatter UV radiation. They contain zinc oxide and/or titanium dioxide as the active ingredients.

Why choose a mineral (inorganic) sunscreen?

Mineral sunscreens are typically less irritating to skin and are considered safer than organic sunscreens.

Chemical sunscreens have a higher rate of allergic reactions in users and some of them are suspected of being disruptive to hormones such as estrogen. Additionally, some of these ingredients (oxybenzone) leach the coral reefs of their nutrients and bleach them white, as well as disrupt the development of fish and other wildlife.

Why zinc oxide is the best mineral (inorganic) sunscreen choice.

Zinc oxide is a much more effective sunscreen than titanium dioxide. It is a better absorber across more UV wavelengths than titanium dioxide. This means zinc oxide provides better UVA/UVB protection than titanium dioxide.

Zinc oxide is the only sunscreen active ingredient that's generally recognized as safe by the FDA for use on babies under six months of age for the purpose of diaper rash cream.

Zinc is a critical mineral nutrient that you often find in vitamin supplements.

Zinc oxide has several properties which make it therapeutic to the skin and useful for certain skin conditions. It is antiseptic, astringent and absorbs moisture, which makes it particularly good for severe eczema. It also helps the skin stay dry when exposed to alkaline liquids – which is why it's used in diaper rash cream. Additionally, it is approved by the FDA as a Category I skin protectant and is used as a soothing preparation for facial redness and steroid-induced thinning of the epidermis.

How long will it take for you to burn if you are wearing sunscreen?

1) First, take the number of minutes you would normally burn in the sun without protection. (Depending on one's skin type and severity of the sun, it only takes an average of 4 to 10 minutes (depending on UV index) for most people to burn from the sun without protection. Sunburn may take hours to actually appear on the skin which means damage is occurring before you can actually see it.)

2) Multiply that number by the SPF of your product. For example, with an SPF 30 x 6 minutes of sun time before burning = 180 (3 hours) ... this is how many minutes you can stay in the sun without burning. If you properly apply an SPF 30 sunscreen prior to sun exposure and you reapply at least every two hours after swimming or sweating.

Fair skin that burns without sunscreen in 4 minutes

1) Apply 30+ sunscreen 15-30 minutes before sun exposure.
2) You have 120 minutes of time in the sun before burning

begins.

3) Reapply sunscreen approximately every two hours or after swimming or sweating.

Fair to medium skin that burns without sunscreen in 6 minutes

1) Apply 30+ sunscreen 15-30 minutes before sun exposure.
2) You have 180 minutes of time in the sun before burning begins.
3) Reapply sunscreen approximately every two hours or after swimming or sweating. This boosts the effectiveness of the sunscreen for the remaining hour.

Medium to dark skin that burns without sunscreen in 10 minutes

1) Apply 30+ sunscreen 15-30 minutes before sun exposure.
2) You Have 300 minutes of time in the sun before burning begins.
3) Reapply sunscreen approximately every two hours or after swimming and sweating. This boosts the effectiveness of the sunscreen for the remaining three hours.

When do you need to reapply sunscreen?

Re-application is necessary and recommended every two hours or as needed, and after swimming, sweating, or towel drying. Use a water-resistant sunscreen if swimming or sweating. Re-application of sunscreen **ONLY** gives the first application a boost in effectiveness, it does **NOT** prolong the amount of time you can stay in the sun.

This means that if you are fair skin, you cannot stay in the sun more than 120 minutes no matter how many times you reapply sunscreen. You need to get out of the sun or cover up with clothing if you don't want to photoage and damage your skin.

What about the importance of Vitamin D?

Up to 85% of adults in the US are believed to be Vitamin D deficient. To know if you are, have your doctor perform a Vitamin D test (aka: the 25 (OH) D Test). If you are severely Vitamin D deficient, consult with your physician about supplementing with higher doses of Vitamin D.

Since most people's Vitamin D source comes from casual sunlight exposure, it is important to supplement your diet with Vitamin D if you are wearing sunscreen regularly.

A lot of food and pasteurized milk is fortified with synthetic Vitamin D. However, many health practitioners believe this type of Vitamin D is much less effective than naturally occurring Vitamin D. Therefore, when possible opt for natural sources like halibut, carp fish, mackerel, eel, salmon, whitefish, swordfish, rainbow trout, cod liver oil, sardines, tuna, eggs, raw milk, and portabello and maitake mushrooms exposed to UV light.

Tricia's Special Offer

Now you know how sunscreen works and just how important it is to wear a mineral sunscreen on a daily basis. As my special gift to you, I would like to send you a FREE Suntegrity face sunscreen sample so you can experience first-hand just how amazing a zinc oxide based, broad spectrum SPF 30 mineral sunscreen can be.

Here is how you redeem my special offer:

1) Go to my website: www.SuntegritySkincare.com
2) Click on "Sample/Travel" from the menu
3) Add one "Deluxe Sample Tube – Natural Moisturizing Face Sunscreen/Primer" to your cart
4) Enter promo code: MCM2017
5) Choose free shipping, check out, and receive your free Suntegrity sample.

Limit one per customer. Offer only valid for customers with a US shipping address.

Tricia Trimble

Tricia is a certified esthetician and the founder of Suntegrity Skincare, an eco-chic, award-winning, safe and natural, mineral sun care line that has grown from a home-based business into a million-dollar sun care company.

She created Suntegrity as a safe sunscreen in honor of her mom, who passed away from melanoma skin cancer. It was her way of keeping her mother's memory alive while helping others stay safe in the sun. Suntegrity products made the EWG's 2017 list of best sunscreens, were featured in several top magazines like Time, Health, Prevention, Allure, and InStyle and won various awards, including a 2013 Best of Beauty Award from Allure Magazine in the Natural Wonders category for their Face Sunscreen & Primer SPF 30. Tricia holds a master's degree in Spiritual Psychology with an emphasis in Consciousness, Health, & Healing from The University of Santa Monica. She founded and ran an online beauty and wellness boutique that promoted inner and outer beauty and worked as a personal development coach to help clients lead more fulfilling and meaningful lives. While running her online boutique, she realized just how important it is to wear safe, natural sunscreen on a daily basis and set out on a journey to create one she loved to wear.

Prior to entering the health and wellness industry, Tricia started her career as a CPA and worked for large corporations like KPMG and Sony Pictures Entertainment and was a founder/partner of Search Finance Group, an executive recruiting firm in downtown Los Angeles.

Chapter 7

How to Live Your Dream Year
by Adaku Ezeudo

Can you imagine living every year as if it was your dream year? Imagine moving to that dream city, writing that dream book, becoming an international speaker or saying goodbye to that soul-sucking corporate job to become an entrepreneur. Guess what? It is possible.

I believe that every one of us is gifted with a dream waiting to be birthed. It doesn't matter how far-fetched it seems or how disappointing the journey has been so far. One thing I know is that it is possible to live your dream and live it every year.

I was born and raised in Lagos State, Nigeria, and growing up an only and eldest daughter with three brothers came with high expectations and responsibilities. It meant that as the 'Ada', I had to be a good role model for my siblings, take on a number of domestic roles, and act as a second mother to my brothers. Even before my teenage years, I took the role so seriously that it extended beyond my family. I soon realized that I enjoyed helping people and putting a smile on their faces. When I went out with my parents and I saw people begging on the street, my heart would break to the point that I cried. It broke more when I saw mothers with their babies pleading with us to help save their sick babies. I even saw young girls, the same age as me, running towards cars, desperately tapping on the side windows of vehicles at traffic lights. I would always nag my parents until they gave these people something, no matter how small. As I got older and had some pocket money of my own, I would often reach out to those down on their luck, particularly women, children, and the disabled, and shared my pocket money with them. At some point, I began to dream that one day I would be able to do more for the less privileged so they could have a permanent smile on their faces.

As I grew older, I set out to begin a career prescribed by my father: accounting. You probably feel that being an accountant is a great job, right? Well...not for me. Despite the fact that I graduated with a second class upper, I did not see any future in accounting for me. I found it boring and incongruent with my vivacious personality. While I'm sure it is a dream for many, for me, it was a nightmare.

My father meant well when he chose my career path. He believed accounting was a valuable degree to possess and it would open doors of opportunity for his 'Ada'. I will always appreciate his choice for me because I have gained invaluable skills as a result of it. The experience helped me discover who I am and empowered me to share my story today. However, despite my years working in the corporate sector both in Nigeria and in my new home, Ireland, I did not have any sense of fulfillment. My corporate career was snuffing the life out of me. I had to make a tough decision to leave a top investment company in Ireland to become a life & career coach, inspirational speaker, and social entrepreneur.

For the past seven years, I have been working with women, helping them on their journey to uncover what's holding them back so they can live their dream, not just today, or this month, but every single year.

I have outlined six steps that helped me on my journey to live my dream; I know they will help you, too. These steps will make you think, help you make decisions, and compel you into action.

1. Dare to Dream

Nothing today has been birthed without dreams. Just as plants cannot grow without a seed, so also, success cannot be achieved without first dreaming. Some dreams seem impossible at first, but when we take that leap of faith, it becomes inevitable.

Throughout history, we have seen the evolution of technology which has allowed people to walk on the moon. This would not have been accomplished without the audacious dreams and unrelenting vision of people like you and me. Even the Bible says, "Where there is no vision, the people perish."

I know you may be asking, "How can I ever achieve my dreams when I am in debt?" or "Where will I ever find the money, connections, or time to make my dreams reality?" You know what? I never had the money or connections, but I was willing to share my dream everywhere I went. In talking about it, I met people who were happy to introduce me to people in similar fields or those who could support my dream.

I never had all the answers, for a time I couldn't even figure out the name of this new career; I just had a story about what I wanted to do. One thing that helped me know I was on the right path was the response I got from people whenever I shared my story. Many told me, "Your eyes light up when you talk about what you do." Others said, "I can see your passion as you speak." I did not know how my body language said it all. I learned that when you love what you do, it shows.

2. Wake up & Take Action

It's easier dreamt than done. So many people have slept away their dreams. They wake up basking in the euphoria of their dreams so much that they don't take action. Many have forgotten it's not the number of hours you spend dreaming that matters, but the number of hours you have woken up to act on your dreams. They keep replaying the dream time and time again, yet nothing is done to fulfill it. Successful people are not lazy; to make your dream a success, you can't afford to be either.

What you do after identifying your dream determines what result you get. I was willing to take calculated risks to achieve my dreams. I left my corporate job only after I had secured another source of income that would keep me going and give me the time to pursue my dreams.

Once I had set myself a task that would bring me closer to my dream, I prioritized it and set to work on it immediately. I prayed to God for guidance, I was laser-focused, educated myself even more to get more clarity, worked late, and was never afraid to ask for help.

Many people's dreams have been quashed because of lack of action. They simply failed to act on what they dreamt about. Taking action can be stressful and demanding, but, trust me; it's worth it in the end.

3. Stay Fearless

One of my greatest strategies is to feed my faith and starve my fear. I have learned to replace the world "if" with "when" because the former suggests doubt or uncertainty while the latter has a positive undertone. When pursuing your dreams, you'll experience a lot of setbacks, disappointments, and pain, but in the face of all of these, you need to stand your ground and remain unshakeable—even when the dream seems to be falling apart. In the process, you will discover a lot of internal strength that you never knew existed. No one conquers with fear; only the fearless succeed in battle.

Growing up, I stuttered as a child. This knocked my confidence. When I decided to follow my dreams to become an inspirational speaker, I was inspired to seek support. It was never easy, but I was determined to stay fearless. I learned different breathing and relaxation techniques that helped me speak more fluently. Some days, I got stuck on my words when speaking in public, but, other days, I did amazingly well. I focused on the positive outcomes and continually practiced and prepared myself before every speaking engagement.

When I planned to leave my corporate job to set up a charity organisation and later a social enterprise, it was very scary. Despite the fear, I did it anyway. I trusted my gut and followed my intuition. I had to turn a deaf ear to naysayers and negative people who could have derailed me early on.

If you quit chasing your dreams because of your fears when will you stand up and succeed? It looks easy when people mount the podium and talk about their success, but it's also important to know that in many situations, they had to stay fearless. They didn't hide when it came to dealing with tough situations.

4. Lead from the Inside Out

If you are empty on the inside, the outside will not be devoid of emptiness. If we focus on nourishing our mind, heart, and soul it is reflected on the outside. Whether we engage in personal development or make healthier choices, continual success can only be achieved when we align the inside and outside of our lives.

I always show up to serve. I ask myself these questions each day: what one thing can I do to serve humanity today? How can I become a better me?

When you lead from the inside out:

- You have humility
- You are teachable
- You are willing to serve others
- You are grateful

I also invest in my personal, spiritual, emotional, and physical growth. While it's great to inspire and influence others, we must begin with one's self first. It's only when we take care of ourselves that we can truly inspire others to do the same.

5. Make an Impact

Can you name a successful leader who hasn't made an impact on the lives of others? In maximizing and fulfilling your dream, you will have to make an impact on others. Trust and belief in a person grows out of recognition of the positive impact they make.

Making an impact is about making a difference, delivering excellence, and transforming lives. It's about listening to the needs of the people you are serving and offering exemplary service that will transform their lives. When I organised a Christmas party for asylum seekers who had made Ireland their new home, I asked them what I could do to put a smile on their face, to make them feel welcomed and valued. The answer surprised me; all they wanted was a visit from Santa for their kids. Sometimes, the littlest things make the greatest impact. What you do for people leaves an indelible mark on them years after you have left them.

There are 8 ways to become a person of influence:

- Live by integrity
- Be a good listener

- Genuinely care for people
- Believe in them
- Network with others
- Empower people
- Show empathy
- Reproduce other leaders

6. Build Your Dream Career

I built my dream career because I dared to dream and act on my dreams. Years after I left my corporate job, I am now an inspirational speaker and run a successful coaching and consulting practice. All this didn't happen by accident. I focused on what I loved doing, put in the hard work, stayed focused and resilient, prayed often, and stayed positive all the time.

No one will build your career for you. Once you have started making progress, remember, it's still not time to stop. You need to keep growing. The moment you stop growing, it means you are dead. Knowing this will help you after you have successfully built the empire of success you always imagined. Expand your imagination each time, widen your scope. Nothing should stop you now. See you at the top.

Adaku Ezeudo

LIVE YOUR DREAM YEAR
WITH ADAKU EZEUDO
Inspiring you to achieve the success you deserve

Get ready to create a life you love so you can make an impact, fulfill your purpose and live your dream.

Got to: http://www.achieveinspiringsuccess.com to find out now.

To book Adaku as a speaker or schedule a consultation, go to:

www.adakuezeudo.com

I look forward to helping you.

Adaku Ezeudo

PS - Get my Free Gift - 6 Powerful Habits that turn your Dreams to Reality.

Go to: http://www.achieveinspiringsuccess.com to get yours now.

Adaku Ezeudo

Adaku Ezeudo is a certified life and career coach, a social entrepreneur, and a transformational speaker. She uses her personal stories to inspire others to become their best selves. She has received multiple awards and recognition for her work on integration, social inclusion, women empowerment, and community leadership since 2009.

Adaku has a background in accounting and holds two Master's degrees, one in Development Studies and another in Business Administration. She founded a charity organization in 2013 to inspire women to grow to their fullest potential and has an intimate understanding on how to help women achieve their personal and professional goals. She is passionate about helping women activate their dreams so they can fulfill their life's purpose.

To book me for TV go to: www.AdakuEzeudo.com.
To book me for a speaking opportunity go to:

www.AdakuEzeudo.com.

Chapter 8

What is Your Truth?
by Catherine Athans, Ph.D.

*Three things cannot be long hidden: the sun, the moon, and
the truth.*

--Buddha

Even as a child, I had a desire to know the Truth—the highest
levels of Truth. I looked for truth from all teachings, and I set
out on a quest to learn from as many different perspectives as
possible.

My desire to know Truth, to find Truth, has led me to the
deepest places in my soul and sometimes the gut-wrenching
darkness of my being. It has led me to the greatest heights and
ushered me into amazing realms and dimensions. It has shown
me infinite possibilities and opened my willingness to know
beyond what words might express. Through these journeys, I
have learned to have a profound compassion and respect for
the human spirit.

My quest has led me to study and be with those who practice a reverent seeking and teaching—from seekers of wisdom

to professors of science; from world leaders to tribal chiefs; from kahunas to professors of medicine and the clergy.

Part of my reason for sharing my understanding and my journey is to give you a means to enter this path of self-discovery in a step-by-step manner. As I gained the knowledge, recognized the Truths, and allowed the Truths to be active in my life, truth then unleashed great joy, love, and prosperity.

The wonders that occur by allowing truth to exist, to be nourished, to expand and then take over are like the brilliant fireworks on Independence Day. This process of *allowing* starts chain reactions of energy within the self and the soul, which then creates openings where once there were walls. It dissolves blocks where darkness previously existed, allowing light to prevail.

The significance of allowing truth in your life, and letting Truth be your mantra, is that you will change in ways you could never imagine. Your thoughts and feelings will give you joy instead of misery. You will soar and enjoy the ecstasy of Truth and let go the pain of lies. Truth has been said to exist in many places.

Through my therapeutic and private healing practices, I have been privileged to travel with my clients to unexplored realms of reality where a new worldview emerges. With courage and hard work, they gain a new idea of who and what they are. It is a marvelous dance full of wonder and magic!

As I see my clients putting into practice the Truths and principles presented here, I am compelled to make the same available to all who wish to seek. In my quest, I have discovered the difference between Truth and lie:

1. **Truth Fills. Lie empties.**
   When you allow yourself to be with, you begin to feel full, whole, peaceful, and free.
2. **Truth loves. Lie fears.**

When you are told the truth, and, when you speak Truth, you feel the love.

3. **Truth nourishes. Lie sickens.**
   You begin to know Truth when you look outside and see a beautiful flower. You simply feel good looking at the flower. That's Truth.

4. **Truth is friendly. Lie is your enemy.**
   You begin to know Truth when you turn the corner and someone notices you, smiles and says, "Good day." That lovely feeling you have is Truth.

5. **Truth guides. Lie misleads.**
   You begin to know Truth when you are willing to go inside and listen to your heart.

6. **Truth is more than intuition.**
   You begin to know Truth when you are willing to take action guided by your intuitive feelings.

7. **Truth sees clearly.**
   You can look at any seemingly negative event and see the Truth that can inspire and propel you to be greater.

8. **Truth is peaceful.**
   When you tell yourself the Truth, you create peace of mind.

9. **Truth feels good.**
   With Truth, your heart automatically opens, giving you more insight, information, and joy.

10. **Truth is happy.**
    With Truth, you feel a lovely sense of anticipation and enthusiasm for your adventures throughout your whole life.

11. **Truth is refreshing.**
    When you are willing to hear, feel, and see Truth, every cell in your body is energized with new life.

12. **Truth creates health.**
    Speaking the Truth activates all of your immune systems, restoring your natural health.

13. **Truth opens your path.**
    When you allow Truth to lead you, the blocks that you thought were there, disappear.
14. **Truth develops courage.**
    You begin to know Truth when you allow yourself to go inside and let go of the lie.
15. **Truth stands by itself.**
    Lie needs to deceive. Whenever you encounter the negative and fill it with love, it transmutes into truth.

Truth is the property of no individual, but is the treasure of all.

—Ralph Waldo Emerson

The Role of Imagination

WHEN SEEKING TRUTH, please remember to allow your imagination to be very large, in full color and in full movement.

Imagination is the act or power of forming mental images of what may not be actually present or what may not have actually been experienced.

Imagination is more than a faculty of the mind. It is a flowing, intuitive gift. It is the ability to see what could be.

Imagination is bringing into being—from little or nothing—great riches.

It is the first tool that you need to manifest, to create your truth.

The process of imagining provides you with an avenue to have greater participation in your own life, for it is your imagination, your thoughts, which create your perceptions of the world in which you live.

Think of this. YOU are the one perceiving YOUR world.

Because of this, you are the one who may change your perception. Imagination is a key in doing this. Taking the time to activate your imagination is key to obtaining what is true for you in your life.

Take a different path

Right now, you have the ability, through your imagination, to choose how you will respond. For example, perhaps you and your employer interact in ways that leave you feeling stressed.

Or perhaps certain exchanges between you and a friend, your partner, your child, or your parent leave you feeling powerless, weak, or dissatisfied. You want to experience encounters which result in different outcomes.

THE CHANGES WILL OCCUR!

Please know that the changes are now occurring even if they are not currently visible to you.

Let's apply this to an actual situation in your life:

Take a moment now and explore a few ways that you can immediately effect change by using your imagination.

DEVELOP A VISION of yourself acting in a way that you want to act in your next encounter with your boss or a family member.

Next, use your physical senses as a starting point toward building a stronger imagination.

ENVISION what you are wearing, see yourself sitting at your desk or at a table.

What you would like to happen in this encounter? BE SPECIFIC and FOCUSED.

What would bring you joy, happiness, or peace?

Now, reinforce your imaginative thoughts by taking physical action:

WRITE down the words you are using in this encounter with your boss or family member while you are calm, cool, collected and intelligent.

Now develop a vision of how you are going to feel in your next interaction with this other person. Focus.

FEEL what it's like to have your emotions in a place that *you* have chosen.

TRUST that what you are imagining from your heart is being created as you are imagining it.

Make time to go inside and experience what it is you are truly feeling, for from every interaction, you have an opportunity for growth.

B r e a t h e .
R e l a x .

Give yourself permission to acknowledge stuck energy and then activate your imagination to get unstuck.

Use your imagination
to paint a different picture,
to write a different script,
to change your position,
to transmute your feelings.

Through your imagination, picture in your mind what it is that you want in your life.

Allow the ideal situation to form pictures in your mind and place yourself in those pictures.

Give them texture and color.

This is the starting point for change.

It may take a little time for the changes to occur, but don't lose heart.

Please take a moment and consider the following:

Nothing exists that wasn't first imagined.

Intuition is greater than knowledge.

—Albert Einstein

The Role of Intuition

Intuition is defined as the direct perception of Truth.

The person who lives life through intuition lives in a state of Truth and in a state of grace.

Intuition allows one to defy the three-dimensional laws and allows things to manifest that may appear to be seemingly impossible.

Using your intuition is key in knowing Truth and creating a sense of joy.

Another key to amplifying Truth is to allow your intuition to have free reign. So often intuition is ignored for something that we deem more reasonable. We tend to honor logic and demean intuition.

However, life does not operate logically.

Logic often leads one down a path of lie.

As you become more familiar with how your intuition feels inside, you begin to use it more.

As you begin to allow yourself to feel what Truth feels like, pay attention to your whole body and see and feel the changes it is making as you do this.

Intuition can be a thought or feeling that literally comes to you out of the BLUE.

The BLUE is the great sea of source from which all things come. It can also be part of your inner guidance that you call upon when making decisions.

Have you ever wanted to find out some piece of information and you turn the corner, look up at the sign, and get your answer?

Out of the BLUE is literally out of the vast, infinite source of life. It is responding to your sincere, truthful desire to Know.

- Do you ever have a sense about something that really can't be explained? That is your intuition.
- Do you ever have a gut feeling about something? That is your intuition

It is vital to allow your intuition to be active and available in your life.

It is the foundation that allows you to experience, see, feel, and know Truth.

Give yourself permission to be with your intuition. Allow yourself to know Truth.

Rather than love, than money, than fame, give me truth.

–Henry David Thoreau

The Role of Discernment

Discernment is a powerful tool to assist you in knowing what is true for you.

To discern is to perceive or recognize one thing from another—to develop your insight, your knowledge, your intuition, and your recognition of the differences and shades of differences and shades of differences in the choices that are presented to you daily.

To discern is to separate Truth from untruth.

Using discernment, you are able to search and know the fine nuances and differences between that which is the precious Truth and that which is the lie that deceives.

Actively using your imagination and your skill of discernment, you receive the Truth of your heart's desires, and you are able to manifest the Truth in all your mind, body, and affairs.

Every cell in your body communicates with every other cell.

Every cell in your body tells the Truth.

What Can You Expect?

Developing your skill of knowing Truth teaches you which possibilities resonate as harmonious for you. When you practice knowing Truth, you begin to open and discover new parts of yourself. You learn who you are and know when you are being true to yourself. As you continue this inner journey, you discover more and more facets of Truth. You become that amazing kaleidoscope of infinite colors, textures, and dimensions.

Please take a moment now to give yourself permission to be with Truth.

How does it feel to allow Truth into your life?

Catherine Athans, Ph.D.

If you are willing to live your life through TRUTH instead of LIE, thus enabling you to achieve real freedom, peace and harmony, then contact Dr. Athans, who can guide you.

Catherine Athans, Ph.D.
www.catherineathansphd.com
www.angelsisland.com
650-948-1796

To receive your FREE booklet on TRUTH, click the link below.

www.catherineathansphd.com/TRUTH

"Dr. Catherine Athans reminds us that Love is the most powerful force in the Universe! Through her loving, caring words, she crafts a plan that works to help the seeker find the Truth to bring health, wealth, and happiness—right now!"
—JOHN GRAY, Ph.D., author of *Men are From Mars, Women are From Venus*

Dr. Catherine Athans

Dr. Catherine Athans' mission is to unlock, encourage, and coach you to actualize your inner power. She helps you uncover and dissolve self-defeating behaviors that have held you prisoner for your entire life. You will discover what is you and what is not you. These differences can be very subtle. With Dr. Athans' assistance, you will begin to know your own truth.

Dr. Athans is a doctor of Clinical Psychology and Health Psychology. She practices in the state of California in San Francisco and Los Angeles. Her experience as a scientist and a compassionate metaphysician allows her the unique ability to offer a myriad of both conventional and unconventional services to her clients.

A moving and dynamic speaker, Catherine has presented and taught at the Global Peace Initiative of Women—a conference inspired by the Millennium Global Peace Summit at the United Nations—as well as the Women's Spiritual Conference held at the United Nations in Geneva, Switzerland. She is a recipient of the President's Special Recognition Award for those who choose to search out innovative systems to serve humankind.

Dr. Athans is the author of six books. Her book, *The Heart Brain,* won an award for Science at the Benjamin Franklin Awards in New York.

Chapter 9

3 Steps to a Loving Relationship and a Loving Life
by Vanessa Standard

Are you sick and tired of making things worse every time you open your mouth or attempt to communicate with your partner or spouse? Do you feel like the harder you try to fix things, the worse they get? Do you want to give up on any of your relationships in order to avoid the inevitable conflicts?

I get it. I suffered for many years. My marriage was a living hell until I was able to take responsibility for my own behavior, identify how I was creating conflict, and change the way I approached my relationship so that I could come from a place of loving rather than blame and judgment.

I finally realized, after much trial, error, pain, upset, and daily frustration that I must stop focusing on what I don't want in my life and in my relationships and start focusing on what I do want in my life and in my relationships. So, I came up with a 3-step system that not only helped save my marriage, but allowed me to create great relationships with others as well. And that is when my quality of life soared and went from an okay life to having a miraculous life with miraculous relationships.

Step 1: Creating Your Ideal Relationships, Creating Your Ideal Life

With whom would you like to see a shift in relationship?

How would you like this relationship to look in a year from now?

Note: This can be a relationship with anybody - your spouse, significant other, family member, friend, colleague, boss, employee, etc.

If your relationship with this person were ideal, what would it look like?

How would you be speaking to each other?

How would you feel when you're around this person in this ideal situation?

What are some of the interactions or exchanges you might have with this person?

How would it be different than it is right now?

How could this relationship bring you the most joy?

What would be the most important characteristics of this relationship? Is it being heard by the other person, or is it that you want the other person to actually feel heard?

What are the missing links in that relationship?

Start by writing down at least ten items that describe how you would like this relationship to look. Using affirmative language, write down these sentences—here are some examples:

1. I am happily communicating with _____.
2. I am feeling so much joy inside my body when I interact with _____.
3. I am expressing myself freely and feeling like I'm heard and

appreciated by _____.

4. I am feeling a heart-felt connection with
_____.

5. I am appreciating how well _____
and I are getting along now.

6. I am finding myself giving and receiving love,
appreciation, and acceptance in my relationship with
_____, and it feels so good.

Write these sentences down, and read them out loud at least three times each day.

Be an active intender and creator in your relationships and in your life by repeating these loving affirmations.

Envision your life unfolding with love and greatness, just the way you want.

Step 2: Better Understanding Blame & Breaking the Blame Game

Generally speaking, nobody ever wants to be blamed... for anything, and no one benefits (in any way, shape or form) through blaming another person for anything at any time.

What occurs in a relationship when blame is at play?

- Blaming disrupts and ultimately destroys trust—the foundation of any relationship.
- Blaming makes constructive, meaningful dialogue difficult (if not impossible) and greatly reduces the possibility for productive interactions.
- Blame creates a relationship barrier between you and the other person and reduces opportunities for vulner-

ability, openness, reconciliation, understanding, empathy, compassion and love.

- Blame brings poison into the relationship and pushes the person being blamed away. In some ways, it's like a slow death for the relationship.
- In blame, we are essentially loose the other person's ability to hear us.

Blame can be identified when we address the person who has upset us with, "You..."

When we can start learning to give up blame, we can elicit a deeper level of listening from the other person.

Whether that person has actually done something against you, OR you have perceived that they have, how do you speak to them reasonably, without blaming?

Communicating Without Blame

1) Ask clarifying questions, rather than making accusations.
2) Do not insinuate wrongdoing, remembering to give that person the benefit of the doubt.
3) Be vulnerable and express how you feel without suggesting that they have purposely done something to hurt you.

When we are able to temporarily suspend blame and take 100% responsibility for our emotions, miracles start occurring.

It is important to acknowledge that our emotions live in OUR OWN bodies—not in someone else's. Therefore, our feelings belong to us—not someone else!

I know this might be a big pill to swallow. However, once I took this philosophy on as truth, my life changed for the better. And, I often hear from others that they see me as a positive and uplifting person. Truly, all that I am doing is accepting 100% responsibility for how I feel, what's happening emotionally in my own body and letting others "off the hook" by not blaming them—and viola—they think I'm extraordinary.

Funny thing is that I'm just a regular person who has learned how to take actions that result in awesome relationships with others. All I do is follow what I am sharing with you. And, by the way, I'm not perfect. This philosophy is a daily practice for me!

Step 3: Clean Up Your Communication, and Then Prize and Appreciate.

This is the time to practice apologizing without defending yourself. When you defend yourself, it comes off as negative and is generally not well received. No one wants to hear that, although you're really sorry that you did (or said) something unkind, insensitive, or thoughtless, you did it because you were in a crappy mood. You negate your apology when you give an excuse. You're basically saying it happened because of this or that, so it's really okay that you did what you did. You disregard the apology.

You acted like a total jerk. You lashed out at somebody. You said something that wasn't very nice. You used an unkind tone with somebody. You were mean. You flaked on somebody. You didn't show up for an appointment. Go back to that person and make amends. Say, "I'm sorry for my behavior." This is not a time for excuses. This is a time for an apology, and that's all. People don't want to hear excuses; they want to hear authentic, heart-felt communication.

And part of that communication also includes prizing others and appreciating them for their greatness. I don't know anyone who doesn't love hearing positive acknowledgments, especially when those acknowledgment come from those they love and care about.

Find something positive to say about the person (people) you're in a relationship with, as a habit, as a way of being. It is about acknowledging the other person, and acknowledgement can at times feel vulnerable. We don't know how people are going to react or respond to us when we get gushy or mushy. Not everybody is comfortable with being told, "I love you." That's okay, because we want to be more aware of what's in our hearts that we want to communicate, so that we can be truly authentic.

Prizing can be really simple. It doesn't have to be mushy or gushy. Try, "Thank you so much for helping me. I really appreciate you." Just a genuine expression of appreciation and gratitude: "I appreciate you spending time with me today." In order for us to receive, we have to practice giving. And in order for us to be able to give, we have to experience and practice receiving. This will help with your communication skills and will result in loving relationships and a loving life.

Vanessa's Special Offer

Now you have three steps and a new way to look at your relationships. You may have also learned what might be affecting the quality of your relationships.

Start today. Get your relationships on track and begin living your life to the fullest!

Email: Support@VanessaStandard.com to request a link for my **free relationship webinar training** filled with helpful information on how to have awesome relationships and an amazing life!

Vanessa Standard

As a young girl I learned that hard work, commitment, and dedication were the keys to moving out of poverty and into the life I really wanted. At the age of eight, in order to buy myself necessities like clothing and food, I became the neighborhood entrepreneur, selling greeting cards and candy, mowing lawns, walking dogs, washing cars, cleaning houses, and caring for neighborhood children.

During this time, I was living with an abusive, drug addicted stepfather and a severely depressed mother. My siblings and I were constantly verbally abused and terrorized by my stepfather, and my mother was regularly physically beaten by this man. The abuse continued until I was in high school when my mother finally left him.

As I entered into adulthood, I became increasingly angry towards the world, and my relationship with others and myself reflected this anger. But my keen survival instincts kept me moving forward, searching daily for solutions that would help me resolve and ultimately transform my inner misery.

After finishing high school, I supported myself through college and graduated with a BA in Business. I then completed my Master's Degree in Spiritual Psychology from the University of Santa Monica.

Chapter 10

Your Highest Calling:
The Seed of Genius in You

by Yvette McDowell

I'll never forget walking into my first fire station where the environment was more than 99% male dominated, an intimidating experience if I must say. I became a first responder in 1980 as a paramedic adding the title of firefighter several years later. Even though I felt confident in my abilities to do my assignment, little did I know, I was getting ready for the ride of my life!

If you are a woman who doubts her value, you're not alone! You were designed with a unique combination of temperament, abilities, and style, to serve in a profession that chose YOU! You have stepped into a career path, although a noble one, certainly not an easy one. A career that touches the lives of so many, regardless of who they are, where they come from, their gender or socioeconomic status.

Whether you're dragging a fire hose or wearing a holster, I respect and honor who you are, for the role you have taken on as a female first responder.

For 25 plus years, I worked as a firefighter-paramedic with the second half of my career as an assistant city prosecutor, who spent a lot of time in the field. During this time, I discovered, and experienced, the difficulties and challenges female first responders face in these professions. The typical challenges faced by women revolve around confidence, leadership, conflict resolution, communication, and courage. By no means is this list exhaustive of everything, but I have found these to be at the top as the most identified.

This is why I'm on a mission to support and celebrate brave women like you, for the profession you've said yes to, and to help you accelerate your professional and personal life. Society is deprived of your best self when you're not living your highest calling.

With that in mind, in that effort to support you, right here and right now, I've gathered together the top 5 ways to help you stand confident and lead in your feminine power.

1) Stand in confidence knowing who you are
2) Be a leader within your community
3) Communicate with power and purpose
4) Using conflict resolution in the office and community
5) Being courageous in the face of danger

Step One: Stand in Confidence Knowing Who You Are

As someone who was where many of you are, I understand deeply what starts to happen in the workplace as far as confidence goes, especially in a dominate, male environment. You may believe that you've got a handle on this new assignment, and someone comes along and criticizes everything you do, from the way you look to the way you handle your equipment and everything in between. How did that make you feel?

Imagine for a moment, an acting female fire captain responding to an emergency call about a fire in her district. As the first unit on scene, it is her responsibility to assess the situation and communicate with other responding units. Typically, when an officer radio's their assessment of the situation there's an immediate response and check in from the others. But, on this day, there was complete silence. Dead air. Nothing! It was as if she was all-alone. It did not take her long to realize that the silent treatment was because she had been put in a position of authority that was traditionally held by a man.

That young woman, some 25 years ago was ME! I felt a deep sense of sadness, frustration, and downright disrespected. It made me question myself, my capability to handle similar scenarios in the future, if placed in that position again.

At that moment, I vowed that I would never allow anyone to make me feel dishonored, disrespected, and dismissed. It was this incident that inspired me to face head-on why having a healthy self-image is so important to one's sense of worth and one's sense of confidence.

So, let me ask you...Have you ever felt frustrated, ignored, or invisible in your work as a female first responder? How many times have you been passed over for a promotion and ever wondered...Is it because I'm a woman? It's time to know who you truly are.

And that's why it's so important you thoroughly develop your confidence.

Step Two: Be a Leader within Your Community

Think about this: If someone's life depended on it, would someone follow you when you gave a command?

It's been said that leaders are born, but don't believe everything you hear. Leadership is a learned skill; the game is figuring out how to become more.

During a critical incident that gained international media attention, involving multiple victims, all minors, I stepped up to assume the role of incident commander in my role as a paramedic. This role required a lot from me. You're thinking about so many things that must happen quickly when life and death is at issue, while taking into account the preservation of evidence at the scene.

The ability to make great decisions with confidence stands at the core of leadership. People are depending on leaders for guidance, just as ships depend on the lighthouse to direct their path to safety.

Leadership requires a lot from a person; it will make a difference in you and the people you serve. You might be asking yourself, serve? You read it correctly, serve!

No one makes it to the top alone. Let's get realistic about this reality. True leaders know that success requires a team. As a leader, you add value to yourself by adding value to others. You must choose to focus on others with a spirit of tolerance.

How prepared are you for moments that will define you as the lighthouse or the iceberg? The choices you make during times of crisis will define you and let others know what you are made of. These are moments in life where leaders set themselves apart from the rest of the crowd or blend in with the crowd. Make no mistake; defining moments will change you. They will determine whether you move forward as a true leader or fade into the background. Which direction will you find yourself heading. As a leader, you will become your best when you seize the opportunity to create change for the better.

And that's why it's so important that you thoroughly develop your confidence.

Step Three: Communicate with Power and Purpose

Communication encompasses more than verbal expression; it also includes the ability to listen. Learning effective communication skills will enable you to connect faster and easier with every person you engage with, and open up unlimited opportunities, personally and professionally.

It is critical when listening that you not only pay attention to what's said, but how it's told, the use of language, both verbal and non-verbal messages. The ability to actively listen, without stepping on another's attempt to communicate with you, demonstrates a willingness to build rapport and establish a sense of trust in you.

I learned this all too well when my partner and I responded to a call where we encountered a man threatening to commit suicide in his home. I was the first through the door when he opened it, and, to my surprise, he slammed the door shut while holding a gun in his hand putting it to his head. I didn't have time to be afraid because that could have cost me my life as well as his, but I made sure that he knew I was there to see, hear, honor, and offer him help.

After talking with him over a course of 20-30 minutes, he put the gun down on the table and agreed to let us take him to the hospital and get the help he so desperately needed.

Had I not taken the steps to grow my confidence and communication skills, I would not have been able to bring this part of his story to a happy ending.

While being a good communicator requires learning skills, before you open your mouth, what are you thinking? These thoughts can create a disaster in your head. With a few simple techniques, you can turn chaotic thoughts into words having a magical effect.

Remember, listening is going to be the greatest skill you develop as part of your communication arsenal. You may have heard this saying, "You have two ears and one mouth for a reason."

And that's why it's so important that you thoroughly develop your confidence.

Step Four: Using Conflict Resolution in the Office and Community

In conflict, are you the voice of reason, or a reason for everyone to run? Or do they see you as a passive observer? Conflict is not a dirty word; how you deal with it can be.

Regardless of how much training and experience you've had in conflict resolution, conflict is a normal and natural part of life.

Imagine, you've witnessed a racially charged incident and you have been called upon to support a position that's being promoted by a majority of people directly and indirectly involved. I found myself in that situation, taking a position that contradicted the majority, which was not received well.

All disputes contain a mixture of common and conflicting goals. Learning how to separate the two can create the space needed to begin the process of building the foundation for a satisfactory and peaceful resolution. Using the commonalities can also help to bring calm to an already tense situation.

There are multiple ways to resolve problems. This hinges on how the parties perceive and approach the situation. Was it a simple misunderstanding? Were there competing goals? At times, these factors can cause the conflict to escalate and turn a simple misunderstanding into a battle of words or physical altercation. When this happens, someone must become the voice of reason and take proactive steps to resolve the conflict in a constructive way for all parties, which was the position I had to take.

When looking at conflict, the position of the parties involved play a significant role. Conflict among peers will look different than conflict between persons sanctioned with authority and the community, but, no matter the position you find yourself in, resolution and perception hinges on how you approach the situation.

And that's why it's so important that you thoroughly develop your confidence.

Step Five: Being Courageous in the Face of Danger

It takes courage to rise to a higher level, to face the unknown, where there is no guarantee about what will happen when you reach the destination. It takes courage to be different, to think outside the box, to be that lone opinion to the contrary in the face of a defining moment. The higher the level you feel compelled to climb, the more you will find out what you're made of, and this takes courage to face the authentic you.

As a prosecutor, I will always remember having to take a stand contrary to the position of a supervisor I reported to. There are times when we must draw a line in the sand and say it's not okay to go along just to get along, especially when it's your credibility on the line. I simply refused to back down and held my position. It all starts within, knowing whom you are at your core.

Courage doesn't mean you will not be afraid, quite the contrary. It means you will keep going, forging ahead, to do what you were called to do. It takes courage to move forward even though those discouraging you may have more longevity and presumably more experience. Realize not everyone has your best interest at heart. It takes courage to stand up to those superior to you and hold your position.

Courageous people follow their instincts when grounded in sound thinking, even in the face of total opposition. It takes courage to confront those that believe your talents are not an integral part of the bigger picture. This may require you to broaden your sphere of influence.

Society has created a false, unrealistic image of what empowered women are supposed to look and act like. But the truth is not every woman was created to stand in the background in silence. It takes courage to have the freedom to be your individual self with an individual voice.

Being disciplined in your mind takes courage, as you face the danger of getting rid of discouraging images and replacing them with images of the strong, talented, courageous, intelligent woman that you are.

And that's why it's so important that you thoroughly develop your confidence.

Yvette McDowell
Empowering You to Stand Confident and Lead in Your Feminine Power

Wanting to take your career to the next level by stepping into your power and excelling in both your professional and personal life?

If yes, I invite you to apply for a **Leadership Acceleration Session call** where we'll explore where you are on track toward your goals and what may be holding you back from greater success.

Best of all.... it is **FREE**!

To apply for a complimentary session go to:
www.standconfidentandlead.com

Based on your answers, I will send you a perfect next step toward taking your career and life to the next level.

During a Leadership Acceleration Session Call you will...
- Get clear about where you are on track toward your goals and where you need to grow
- Spot places where you may be sabotaging your success at work
- Explore where you would like to be personally and professionally one year from now
- Identify powerful next steps you can take to accelerate your success and experience more fulfillment from your work

I'm excited to be connecting with you, and look forward to being a part of your next level.

Yvette McDowell

Confidence and leadership keynote speaker Yvette McDowell is a former fire-fighter-paramedic and a retired Emmy Award Winning Assistant City Prosecutor whose encore career as a keynote speaker, transformation expert, and workshop leader is to change the game for the better for female first responders from Pasadena to San Diego to Seattle as well as to Police and Firefighting Training Academies everywhere.

Today, Yvette McDowell's essential message to female first responders is "Step Up. Get Busy. Start Leading; and Take Their Game to the Next Level and Get That Promotion Every Time." Her powerful message can transform the culture in your department instantly. Women will walk taller, show up more powerfully, and lead more boldly.

Yvette's keynotes and workshops create paradigm shifts that make policing and firefighting better for all first responders and those they serve. Fools don't rush in when they follow her sound guidance. They stop, think, and take informed, inspired actions. This saves more lives while building stronger rapport with team and the community.

With Yvette as your guide, through her Ultimate Life Transformation System, first responders will learn to take inspired and decisive steps to stand confident and lead in their feminine power so they will begin to really get what they say they want, while reaching for and achieving their dreams.

Connect with me here – www.standconfidentandlead.com.

Chapter 11

Sizzling After 60
by Sally Landau

I was married for 27 years. Somewhere along the line, it spiraled out of the fun zone and became a serious free fall without a parachute. And then, I was single. Divorced. In terms of relationship, alone.

I spend the requisite amount of time healing. You know, that time where you don't know what to call yourself. You're no longer a wife.

It took a while to get divorced....not that I could easily wrap my head around that "D" word. And yet I didn't feel single either.

My weekends provided choices I could make on my own. First, it was movies. My selection. No negotiating involved. The first Saturday night, I went to TWO films back-to-back.... both gritty. Walking out of the theatres, the stories blended into some forgotten memory, and yet, I remember I liked being with *me.*

So, I found things to do each weekend. Many of them new adventures. Through a manicurist's prodding, I began attending Argentine tango classes. No one had warned me how complicated this dance could be. Fascinated, I would hang out after my beginners' class to watch the immediate level folks, so I could see if this was a goal I wanted to achieve.

Soon, I went to three milongas a week (that's tango dancing). And I came to know a new community of friends, but what I really did was dip my toe into the relationship ocean. One dance at a time. These guys, just as nervous as I, attempting to remember not only the steps but also the correct way to lead the woman, put their arm around me. Some held me close.

Occasionally the instructor chose me to demonstrate a new step we must learn. These men, many guest instructors straight from South America, held me so close, our silhouettes blended. Even my breathing had to be in sync with theirs. A few beats and then they'd release me.

Mini dates for a few musical measures.

Let me pose this question: When was the last time a man held you longer than a hug's worth?

Dancing helped me get over a fear I didn't know I had. Closeness. Blouse to shirt. Pressing bodies. And it didn't mean anything. We students, nervous and focused on steps and signals, even attempting this sexy dance, were not wondering "is this chemistry?"

And while I did learn to tango, I learned gobs more about myself. I could be comfortable in a man's arms. I could be patient. I could allow him to lead me around the floor. I could surrender. And I could flirt. Once you understand tango, this dance IS a flirt!

This set me up for dating in ways I couldn't have imagined.

Tango gave me license to look into a man's eyes, smile, laugh, have fun and have it mean nothing. Just a moment shared on the dance floor.

I slid into dating without fear. Would you believe I jumped on five dating websites? I figured where would I, a former co-manager of an architecture firm, be able to sit down with men who couldn't wait to enthusiastically tell me about themselves? This could be fun! And it was!

There was a rapid-fire six months when I went out with 46 first dates. Wonderful men. Okay, so I only had chemistry with six....like the time I walked into a Starbucks to meet a coffee date. The guy smiled at me, and I immediately imagined myself kissing him....perhaps that night.

And then I met a man that just made me feel at home... immediately...at a speed dating event. It also didn't hurt that he laughed when I thought I'd said funny stuff.

On our first date, lunch at The Lobster in Santa Monica, we shared a convivial conversation, and since I'm chatty, I began skipping to several subjects in an attempt to get to know Ken better...to see if I wanted another date with him. I asked him something about his education, and he gave a vague answer and quickly said, "I'm not telling you my age."

Huh? I don't recall asking that. Later, I wanted to know his birth order. Knowing he has a sister, I asked who was older, and again he said, "I'm not telling you my age."

Fact is, when I'd initially met him, I thought he might be younger than me, and while that didn't matter to me, it occurred to me that he, like most men, may want a much younger woman. I stressed about this for the three days it took for us to get to this date. It never occurred to me to check U.S. Search for his information, which was there for the world to see.

When the web was young and forming, I was able to ask U.S. Search to delete my info, so when Ken, concerned I might be way too *young for him*, went directly to that site, we know what he found. Nuthin'.

So, this brings us to the Santa Monica Pier. We have finished a wonderful lunch and are walking toward the water after a spin on their baby roller coaster. I ask one more question, which he figures is more of my persistent prodding about his age, and he stops. He once more says he's not telling me his age, and it occurs to me to do something I've never done before.

I say, "Wait a second. NOW this age thing is becoming a THING. Let's just get it over with and tell each other our ages." He blanches ever so slightly, and then his gentleman comes forth, and he says, "You first." I tell him a number, which is four years his junior. First, his jaw drops. Then his confession to me, and my jaw drops, and spontaneously, I spurt, "Let's just get the first kiss out of the way too," and I plant a big one on his ample mouth. Sealed with a kiss.

THAT marked the beginning of our relationship. It set a tone of playfulness. And I felt I could be myself with this guy... totally myself.

Soon we see each other four times a week, then five days and nights. His place on the weekends, and after I move from the married BIG HOUSE, it's almost every night in my little rental. A whirlwind of months fly by, and we move into a house. Our house. A house to share. A life to share. And some of it becomes routine. Grocery trips, meals to make, dishes to wash, dogs to walk. Are you showering first, or am I?

We spent six years together, and then, I married Ken, date #45. He's Husband #Last. And all that began in 2003.

I don't want this relationship to become routine. I want each day fresh, full of wonder and surprise. Ok, I like that Ken is a good cook and has pretty much allowed me the princess role of waiting till meals are served and me sauntering to the table when called. THAT routine, that one's nice. But the rest of it? I want the magic to continue, and I'm happy to do my part.

C'mon, we all know relationships are a multi-faceted, constant cycle of giving and receiving. It's not always in perfect balance, but as my grandma Florence said, "It all shakes out."

What happens when *you* face disputes? Some people, when they get pissed off, can only think about winning an argument. I truly believe that a relationship's long-term success may hinge on a couple's ability to resolve them.

And most of us have heard the old adage: "You want to be right or happy?"

Keeping my mind and my emotions wrapped around my goal of maintaining and deepening this relationship, I cannot be focused on winning. Ahhh, winning arguments feels so good....in the moment...like chowing down on a second helping of gooey lasagna or eating a huge dessert. But how do I feel the next day?

If I insist on winning arguments with someone I love, then that makes them the loser. Being in love with a loser is not my goal.

No, it's not about winning. It's about informing. Rather than focus on winning an argument, I could teach Ken how to get along with me better....should this issue arise again.

I won't let immediate frustration or anger blindside me into forgetting I love this man. I could reach deep into my toolbox and pull out fun, love and humor. And not sarcastic humor. Sarcasm may, in the moment, demonstrate how clever I am, but it doesn't further a relationship or draw people closer together. My goal is to achieve intimacy.....not encourage distance.

I like to say Ken is linear in his thinking. Most of the time, he's a straight line. And I'm squiggly. So, when he has "suggestions" for me, when he offers a better (translate HIS) way to accomplish something that I know I will not be able to do, I answer, with a laugh or a smile:

"I have many fine qualities; this isn't one of them."

A little humor, some soft love, but more important, **I've let him know that I heard him**. I've acknowledged him.... *and* I'm standing my ground.

I can also speak to him in a playful, non-threatening way that he will understand. For example, if I'm frustrated, I might say while pointing to below my waist:

"When you talk to me like that, this turns into the Sahara Desert." His face shines, and he smiles.

This has worked so well, for a few of our early years, I could employ code words. Simple things like: "Sahara!" or "Desert!" That lovely secret language communicative couples develop and cherish. I realized disputes might arise, and I wanted to handle them effectively.

So, while we're talking about sex, and not *realllly* withholding it, I want to remember a time being very young, probably seven years old. I thought my parents would never, should never, engage in sex....unless it produced a younger sibling. Otherwise, ick. Even my daughter, as she approached her pre-teen years, blurted, "I can imagine Dad doing that, but YOU?"

And now, I'm actually beyond my parents' age. Having sex. Realizing why my parents did also. And wondering how to keep it fresh. Can we?

I decide there may be ways that I can remind him...maybe if we're both lucky...I could remind him on a daily basis that he is my sexual partner. That I think about him THAT way.

I can flirt. I can be obvious or subtle. When his shoulders are tight or his feet ache, I can rub them. I can look into his eyes longer than expected. For example, when my husband asks what I want for dinner, I can look dreamily and say, "Oh, I know you'll make the best decision and surprise me." I marvel at his vast vocabulary and his ease in beating me at word games. I can be inspired by my paternal grandparents, Joe and Tillie, married more than 60 years, who would reach across that airy divide between their proper twin beds each morning upon waking. They'd stretch their fingertips till touching and say, "We made it another day." I can moan when

Ken returns the back rubbing favors and knows just how to soften my kinks. I can moan other times, too. I can tell him what I'm thinking about him, or send him one of his favorite texts as I'm about to return to our house, "I'm coming home to you."

Yeah, I'm happy to say, older people think like that.

So, what about YOU?

Are you in a long relationship that's fizzling? Do you miss the affection that you once enjoyed? Has sexy time turned into TV binge-watching?

This can happen at any age, with any couple, and it seems to be prominent with partners who've known each other a very long time. We've heard the expression, "the blush has left the rose," so it may not be surprising that after a long time together, couples can become more distant in some ways.... often in intimate ways.

So many things to get us off track: work demands, children, maybe grandchildren needs, fatigue, perhaps some loss of sexual function, distraction and upset from compelling media reports.

We need to remember who this person is in our lives and how much we love them and what we fell in love with in the first place. Don't we want the best for them? Don't we deserve the best for ourselves too? Sometimes we allow day-to-day minutiae of our lives to take precedence over attending to our relationship.

A quick Rx for this is a dose of pausing. Pausing to reflect.

Here's an exercise. Take as long as you like with this, and since it's private, you can alter and add to it at will.

> List the reasons you were attracted to this person in very beginning.
> What drew you to his side?
> What made you want to stay?

> What were the best qualities of this man?
> How many of those do you see today?
> In other words, in his deepest essence, is he the same guy you fell for way back when?

Or, perhaps a completely different scenario – you're not in a relationship and haven't been for a very long time? Perhaps never? And now, you feel older, can barely remember being nubile, notice the power of gravity on your body and feel it has somehow abused you by changing and aging. Or maybe there are other imaginable scenarios in between not mentioned above.

If any of these resonate, here's an exercise for you. Again, this is your private journal. Rewrite if necessary.

> Before that first gaze in the mirror each day, do you still feel like a young woman?
> Do you like to be touched?
> Would you like someone you care about to hold your hand?
> Or perhaps, if touch seems threatening, you want a chance to spend quality time with someone sharing fun experiences.
> Are you craving some love, some attachment... perhaps a great friend to partner with?
> Do you know in the deepest crevasses of your soul that you are smart, interesting and have contributed to the world in small or large ways?
> Now, here's the fun part. Pretend you're in the creative department of a hip advertising agency. Figure out a campaign to sell YOU. List your finest qualities:

- ❖ the ways in which you shine
- ❖ how you are clever, amuse others or yourself
- ❖ things that spark optimism
- ❖ what makes you smile
- ❖ activities you enjoy

And then, write a commercial to promote you to the outside world. Emphasize the positive and also be realistic. Then read it to yourself. Have you painted a picture of someone you want to be? Someone to whom you'd be attracted? When you feel good inside about yourself, you change on the outside and often attract like-minded people. When you believe in yourself, others will feel your confidence. And confidence is sexy.

In long term and new relationships, you can't expect to receive the love you dream about to resurrect or simply knock on your door if you aren't willing to do the work to make it so, and that work begins with feeling good about yourself.

If you're in a long term relationship you see as fizzling, if you still believe there's a foundation worth saving and are willing to do the work, change is possible. And that change begins within.

Have you done the exercises? If not, are you willing to go back and journal the answers? Love is possible when you love yourself first, when you find ways to be playful... and stay focused on moving relationships forward.

Grab a free copy of my gift "How to Create an Ideal Online Dating Profile" at:

www.EasyOnlineDatingProfile.com

You'll Find out that:

> **Lots of wonderful people hunt for relationships on-line.**

> All the good ones are NOT taken.

> **Many of them are looking for YOU!**

> There are a dizzying number of dating websites available on-line and I'll guide you along to the right one for you.

> **The right way to complete your profile.**

> There are plenty of folks like you looking for relationships – and I can help.

Sally Landau

Sally Landau is a California-based dating coach and relationship expert. While not a rocket scientist, or inner city school teacher, she does consider her work important and likes to think of herself as a heart surgeon, in that her sage coaching elevates dating and romance to its rightful place: mysterious, exciting, and essential.

Ms. Landau has chosen to live a happy life, and is a living example of that to her coaching clients. Having majored in psychology, co-managed a prestigious architectural firm, endured more self-help seminars than a sane, adjusted person would ever admit, and been a certified life coach, Sally is expertly positioned to extend her trained hand to women over forty who hate to date and want a mate.

She knows how to help clients love themselves, as she guides them in growing their self-awareness. She has crafted a process where women can genuinely define what they're looking for in a partner, but most importantly, she invites all to consider that the dating journey can be fun.

In her universe, flirting is an example of such fun. It does not have to be sexual. The thought of flirting, or even better, banter, can be a reason to wake up in the morning. There's so much fun in learning to play in the moment.

It's important to Sally that her clients understand that dating is an opportunity to learn more about themselves, and the more you know and embrace and love about you, the more you'll have to give. Sally's dating, a fun-filled trial and error journey and her playful energy, which comes through in the pages of her book, make this a really uplifting read.

To learn more or to connect with Sally:

http://datingcanbefun.com
https://facebook.com/datingcanbefun

Chapter 12

My name is Veronica Anusionwu, and I was born in Lagos, Nigeria. My parents were hard working and had a promising future, but at the age of 5, my father died unexpectedly. Shortly after that, my mother became seriously ill. At a very young age not only did I have to learn to fend for me but also to look after my younger siblings.

Witnessing my mother's constant pain affected me profoundly as a child. I had a consistent and profound longing to find out how I could stop people from becoming ill. Something inside kept rising and telling me that sickness was somehow "wrong," an aberration of the world, but I did not know where that thought came from or why it kept coming back. I did not see at the time that it would be through this firsthand experience of the devastation caused by an illness that God would lead me to dedicate my life to help others overcome sickness and pain.

I must admit that I was stupefied when God called me to teach his people that disease can be crushed and, more particularly, that women and men who have infertility can overcome with the Word of God. If anyone had told me that I would write books on infertility and miscarriage when I was a teenager, I would have never believed that it would be so. In fact, I never thought I would ever write a book, any book for that matter. God called me to write health and healing books, and I have written twenty so far and am still going strong.

My calling to heal infertility

I gave my life to Jesus when I was 27 and was enjoying my new relationship with the Lord when, barely a few days later, I heard God telling me: "You are going to write medical and healing books for me." I was rather shocked since I have no medical background. But I just said "yes" to God. And to my utter amazement, as soon as I said yes to God, suddenly the Bible became a living book for me, and I had the revelation that Scriptures have more power than prescription medication and could be used to cure a variety of ailments when used in faith. At the same time, I also had specific verses come to my mind, and I was able to start writing books immediately. It was as if the Bible was an open book in my heart.

Many people do not know that the promises in the Bible contain healing powers in them. When this knowledge was imparted to me, I immediately started "prescribing" Biblical promises to family and friends who were sick and seeing healing results follow. Then, one day, as I was walking down the road near my house, I found an article that was talking about women having difficulties conceiving at a certain age. This struck me very deeply. An overwhelming sensation of "wrongness" overtook me, just like when I was a child watching my mother suffer. I almost exclaimed out loud: "Lord this does not agree with the Bible." I heard Him in my spirit tell me, "Since you know that's not true, then write a book and correct it." This is how I started writing books about infertility and was led to counsel infertile women and couples. It brought me to the work of my entire life.

I feel compelled to mention here that, if God is speaking to you about doing something big, or you have a feeling in you that something great is in you to do, do not ignore it or be afraid! Do not say, "Oh wow, me!? I can't-do it; I don't know how." Believe in yourself and the goodness, power, and might of the Lord. Believe you can do it and I can assure you that you can, with God's help. I shudder when I think that, had I doubted God, many lives that are blessed today through me would never have been transformed.

Over the years, I have worked tirelessly to serve the Lord faithfully and help families from all over the world welcome children in their womb and their arms. My books and my counsel ministry have touched and changed the fate of men and women in the United Kingdom, Singapore, India, the United States, and Africa. God is as much a miracle worker as He was 2000 years ago.

Over the years, so many amazing testimonies have touched and impacted my life. I will mention four that stand out for me right now:

Asencao Firth

My dear Asencao Firth who was given a .007% chance of having a baby and came to me so wounded and hopeless. After working with her for one year, she embraced a baby son in March 2017, to the glory of God.

Mrs. Antonia Ozoemena
I also have tender memories of Antonia who had her baby at 59, ten years after her menopause! I coached her on how to exercise her faith in God's Word to crush infertility and embrace a child when all had been lost in the physical realm. It was so amazing to see her supernaturally pregnant in the natural world at 58 and having her first son at 59 with God's authoritative Word and my divine coaching!

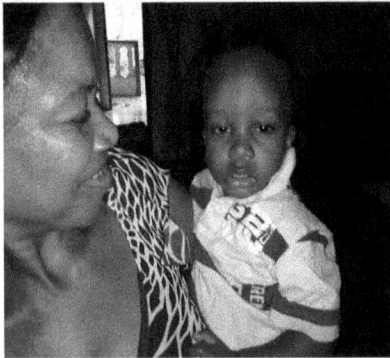

Ify Olatunji

I can also never forget my formidable Ify Olatunji who had her fallopian tubes cut after an ectopic pregnancy. She built her faith relentlessly by attending my faith clinics and dedicating herself to the Word under my supervision and delivered a spirited baby boy a year later. I still laugh when I remember how flabbergasted the doctor was and how he exclaimed: "How is this possible? Did I not cut your tubes myself?!"

Mrs. Chordess Harris

And then there is beautiful Chordess Harris whose husband was diagnosed with a major sperm production problem, Azoospermia. The day she received the news from the doctor that she could never have a child, her husband and she were so distraught that they got lost going home from the medical office. She signed up to work with me, and I told her to destroy the doctor's report and put the Word of God over it. I put a plan in place, and Chordess did not hesitate and became a faith warrior, declaring the Word unceasingly until, through the power of God's Word, she conceived and is now the happy mother of a baby boy and pregnant with another one six months later.

I know how to help you

As a fertility coach specialist working under God's guidance, I go through the disturbing reports, beliefs, and emotions women and couples feel with a fine-tooth comb and help them clear their minds and hearts to let God do His Work in them. That is what I have committed my life to do: bring hope, faith, and healing to those who are not living their best life because they do not know that God wants to give them an abundant life. It is my responsibility to help all those who are suffering from illness and infertility find God's great plans for their lives.

The promises of God cannot fail

Sometimes, I have to take people who come to me by the hand and work step by step with them before they receive their testimonies. This is mostly due to where they are coming from spiritually. It could be caused by different issues, such as their faith or difficulties in trusting God's Word as real. No matter the challenge, I take it up and work through these problems to get their breakthrough. I never give up, but, sometimes, women facing fertility challenges do not focus and keep looking for the next "new" solution. If they "try God" for a month or two and move on to something else, chances are they will not receive their blessing. The Word of God works every time, but one must speak it, believe it, and keep with it day and night. As a counsellor under God's guidance, I stand with whomever God sends my way for the long haul. My goal is to help those who come to me establish a relationship with God that will last the rest of their lives. I do not propose a "fad" fertility diet. I offer what my Master offers: healing to those willing to walk with Him and give their faith to Him.

What I have discovered about the promises of God

The most important thing I have learned by doing God's work in the field of illness is that God has given us so much in His Word to use to overcome diseases and infertility. The Bible promises us great blessings as we walk in faith and trust God. Don't only read your Bible: believe what the Bible says. Literally.

I wish I could impress upon each person who comes in contact with me how strong God's Word is in every situation. My personal experience in God's Word over the years has taught me that God's word is absolutely, completely, unshakably, trustworthy and dependable every time and in every situation. My own family and I have experienced great miracles through the power of God's Word. Whatever it is you might be facing, I want you to know that there is nothing wrong with you or your family. God loves you and will surely bless you with a baby, healing, or prosperity, as He has done for many others. God is incommensurably good. He is Good. Over a period of twenty-two years of helping men and women overcome sicknesses and pain, I have seen the goodness of God over and over and over. The Bible tells us that the earth is full of God's goodness, but many people do not believe this. Not believing does not change what is already there; it just means that, if you do not believe, you are not able to receive and enjoy the goodness of God that is available to you.

I am so glad that God, in His love and mercy, enabled me to believe in His powerful Word and goodness. He also allowed me to share His love with so many people of diverse race and culture and religion. Infertility has no color, no social class, and no boundaries. When people are desperate enough they will do anything to have their baby. They will often explore every possible technique until, often as a last resort, they come to God through me. Some people even say to me, "God is not real, God cannot help me." This is what I say to those who come to me:

"Why not give the Lord a try? How can you make judgments on God's goodness without giving Him a try? It is like saying that the tea is too sweet without tasting it. I want you to know that God loves you and is eager and ready to bless you. All you need to do is reach out and receive His love for you.

"I want to tell you that help is at hand and that you can fulfill your dreams of motherhood. Your desire to have children has been given to you by God Himself and He intends

to fulfill those dreams. God needs those children to come forth through you. Reread this: God needs you to have those children and has already blessed you with them. You do not know this and that is why you hurt and wonder why your hunger for a child is not quenched.

"There is no limit to God's power, and in my walk with God for over 22 years, I have witnessed the birth of hundreds of babies born to men and women who had been deemed infertile by the medical industry. This does not, in any way, take away the respect I have for our great doctors that do a great work in our lives. All I want you to know is that where science cannot help you, then God's power is available for you.

"God has anointed me to teach men and women how to bring forth their children into the world through faith in Him and His unfailing Word. I have faithfully committed my entire life to helping you achieve your goal of having your children and building a healthy and happy family. Through my teaching, coaching, my 'Overcoming infertility books' and powerful faith clinic messages, you will be empowered to open up to God. Also, you will have the knowledge and revelation that He had already answered you, even before you called; and that your children are already in the embrace of your arms, even though you cannot see them physically.

"I love helping people overcome through the promises of God. This is my calling. I love God's Word as it cannot fail and it has the power in it to do what God has promised you.

"I am always ready and willing to do my best to help those who reach out. My coaching and counselling services are all open and available to you. My faith clinics and Sunday services are a source of great divine impartation. Let me help you. Let God help you. Let me teach you how God can help you."

My home life

Even though I am quite busy an author, motivational speaker, fertility coach specialist, founder and Senior Pastor of Lord's Word on Healing Centre (LWH), I am also married and the blessed mother of two wonderful children. I love writing, singing, sewing, cooking and travelling in my spare time, but my most favourite activity is sitting at home with my husband of over 27 years and laughing together at our life and the many blessings it has brought us. My husband should have been a comedian as he knows how to turn everything into laughter. As we grow older, we have found our rest in God and spend a lot of time with our children, joyously giggling and rejoicing in God's goodness.

God bless you and your family.

Veronica Anusionwu

Five habits you can use straight away to start crushing infertility in your life.

Although we can all potentially fall prey to sickness and infertility, the Bible states that these afflictions do not come from God but from the evil powers at work in this world. To free ourselves from the shackles of disease (and infertility is a disease) we must take faith-filled steps daily, if not hourly. We must renew our minds and attitudes constantly, keeping our thoughts captive and learning to face life from a completely different perspective, the perspective of faith. We must consider ourselves the children of God, act according to His Word, and step up to the position he gave us in His Kingdom, right next to Him. He is an amazingly loving Father who has each of us tattooed on the palm of His Hands. Here are five principles that will transform your current situation if you apply them consistently and faithfully.

1. Learn to forgive quickly

You might be surprised to hear that the word of God tells us in no uncertain terms that holding on to resentment and un-forgiveness can lead to a lot of negative things in our lives, including sickness and infertility. God warns us about this in the Bible. If you feel like you cannot forgive in your own strength, ask God and the Holy Spirit to help you. Many women who were infertile for years were able to conceive after they forgave those against whom they bore grudges. *If you forgive those who sin against you, your heavenly Father will forgive you. But if you refuse to forgive others, your Father will not forgive your sins.* Mark 6:14-15. Let go of the past so your womb and your cells can be cleansed and renewed.

2. Learn to stop worrying and minimize stress

The Bible tells us that we should not worry about our situations and our lives but bring all our cares to God. Stress can lead to the breakdown of the body and cause infertility. It is also, indirectly, if you think about it, lack of faith in God that leads to fear and anguish. As Matthey 6:27 asks: *Can any one of you add a single hour to your life by worrying?* Try to find peace and rest in your body. Don't fret about anything; instead, pray about everything. Tell God what you need, and thank Him for all he has done. Then you will experience God's peace, which exceeds anything we can understand. (Philippian 4:6-7). Quashing your doubts with the Word and resisting stress will translate into peace of mind, peace of heart, peace of your cells, and peace of your womb. This peace is essential to healing as well as conceiving.

3. Learn to bless your body

Many of us may never have heard anyone tell us to bless our bodies. But I can assure you that blessing your body and loving it can help you beat infertility. We are just so critical of our figures. We turn our hearts against ourselves and God's perfect creation. We set our bodies to sickness and deterioration because of our constant internal criticism and even hate. Change what you think about your body. Many times, we just forget how faithful our bodies have been and how they deserve our love and care, too. So, go ahead and give it some kind words now. Bless your body with some tender loving words. Remember also that your body is the temple of the Holy Spirit. If you continuously attack your body with your mind and your words, you bind the Holy Spirit who then has very little space to flow within you. Bless every part of your body in the name of the Lord, especially those parts you feel or have been told are defective or less than perfect. Nothing is imperfect. Everything is perfect. Pour love into every cell of your human body. The spiritual will always beat the physical. God's power is unlimited. Unleash the power of blessing through your lips. Speak up and speak out loud. Bless, bless, and bless. And do not stop blessing, do not get distracted by other people's views, reports, or criticism. Your body will be transformed.

4. Learn to watch your words

To beat sickness, disease, and infertility (or a plight of any kind I should add)—you **must** watch your words. And I mean **every** word you speak. The Bible says there is life in the words you speak. There are creative powers in them, too.

So, learn to speak the right words all the time. Don't call up your friends that don't have faith to tell them what the doctors said. My books work so well because in them I teach you how to pronounce the right words all the time for yourself. People are often familiar with Proverb 18:21 that states: *Life and death* are in the *power* of the *tongue, and those to whom it is dear will have its fruit for their food.* **You must take this verse absolutely literally.** Everything you say (and think for that matter) creates. Not only do I urge you to curtail your lips but also go forward and say, say, say, *what you want* and *not* what you see. Do not repeat bad news. Faith is the substance of things hoped for (Hebrews 11:1), and this faith must be expressed through each and every word you speak. Guard your words like a hawk. They are the jewels that will fill the treasure chests of your life and make them overfill. Your words are like medicine to your body and the beating heart of your babies.

5.   Learn to trust God and His Word

Finally, speak and pray the promises of God in faith and believe in them. Many people fail to experience God's love because they do not trust Him. We often have a very distant sense of who God is and what He wants to do for us. I am here to tell you that He wants to bless us in every way possible. And He wants a relationship with us, a very close relationship in fact. He put the Holy Spirit right into our beings so we can talk to Him at all times. Perhaps it sounds easier said than done to "just trust Him", but do you realize how many man-made ideas we have trusted for years if not centuries that were false? We are deluged with fake news, fake studies, and fake science. Nothing can protect us but God's arms. God is not a man that He should lie. (Numbers 23:19). He is *always* there. We are placed on this earth to find our way back to His almighty and tender arms. Psalm 37:3-13 says *Trust in the LORD and do good; dwell in the land and enjoy safe pasture. Take delight in the LORD, and He will give you the desires of your heart.* Trusting God completely does not mean that no man can help you. But it does mean that God can *always* help you completely if you let Him. Bet everything your heart can spare on God and ask Him to build your faith; ask Him to teach you how to rest in Him at all times and in all situations.

So right now, this day, this very minute:

1. Forgive everybody who has ever crossed you
2. Relax and rest on God's promises
3. Bless your body out loud constantly
4. Speak what you hope for in faith (and stop all negative talk!)
5. Lean on Him with all the weight of your soul!

May God bless you richly as you put your trust in Him. Amen!

Feel free to grab a copy of my guide

Help for Infertility, You Can Crush Infertility at Your Age

Go to: WWW.helpforinfertility.com

Free guide you will discover how to:

- Defeat infertility through prayer.

- Become pregnant quickly using Gods WORD.

- Show you that you are not too old to conceive!

- Prayer for a woman facing infertility.

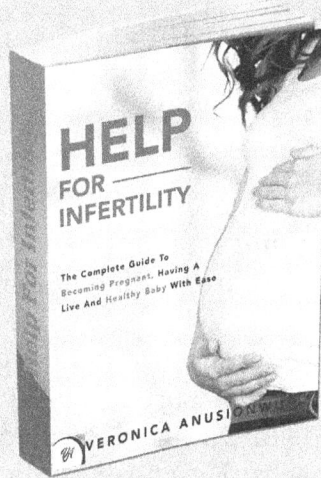

If you want to overcome infertility, change the way you think.

You can have a fresh start.

Get a Free 30 minutes consultation, go to—
Trhttps://tinyurl.com/y6wnsleb

Value $250

Veronica Anusionwu

Veronica Anusionwu is the author of more than twenty books in the fields of healing, infertility, and faith. She has counselled men and women around the world, from America to Africa, for over 22 years and directs a monthly Faith Clinic that she leads at her Healing Centre in London, UK. She also offers various coaching services which have been a source of great blessing to many. She also holds and preaches a Sunday Worship services four times a month and teaches an international Bible study class where participants regularly "Skype" from three different continents.

A motivational speaker, fertility coach specialist, founder of Lord's Word on Healing Centre (LWH), Veronica Anusionwu has dedicated her life to serving the Lord in the capacity He chose for her i.e. as a faith healer. Steeped in her astounding knowledge of the Bible and the Word of God, Veronica Anusionwu brings to everyone she meets the peace and love of God as well as individual, honed-in support and counselling. The miracles that have blossomed thanks to her counselling are wondrous.

Veronica Anusionwu has successfully coached hundreds of families who were deemed infertile by the medical profession who are now holding babies in their arms.

She has brought joy and healing to many families thorough her overflowing love for people.

A Final Note from
Tracy Repchuk

Thank you for your investment in this book, and for the continuing relationship you will have with me and the co-authors.

We are dedicated to serving you and your needs and look forward to our journey together with you.

You can claim all of your free gifts from this book at www. MissionCriticalMessengers.com. Simply enter your order # from Amazon and gain access to where all the author's gifts are located.

Enjoy the journey and stay in touch.

Connect with us on our Facebook page which has a link on your gift download page.

To Your Ongoing Success,
Tracy Repchuk
7-Time International Bestselling Author and Speaker

If you would like to become a published author and be in a book like this with me, go to

www.QuantumLeapAuthor.com

and take your next step.

www.ingramcontent.com/pod-product-compliance
Lightning Source LLC
Chambersburg PA
CBHW050130280326
41933CB00010B/1314